THIS BOOK

Belongs to

I0473102

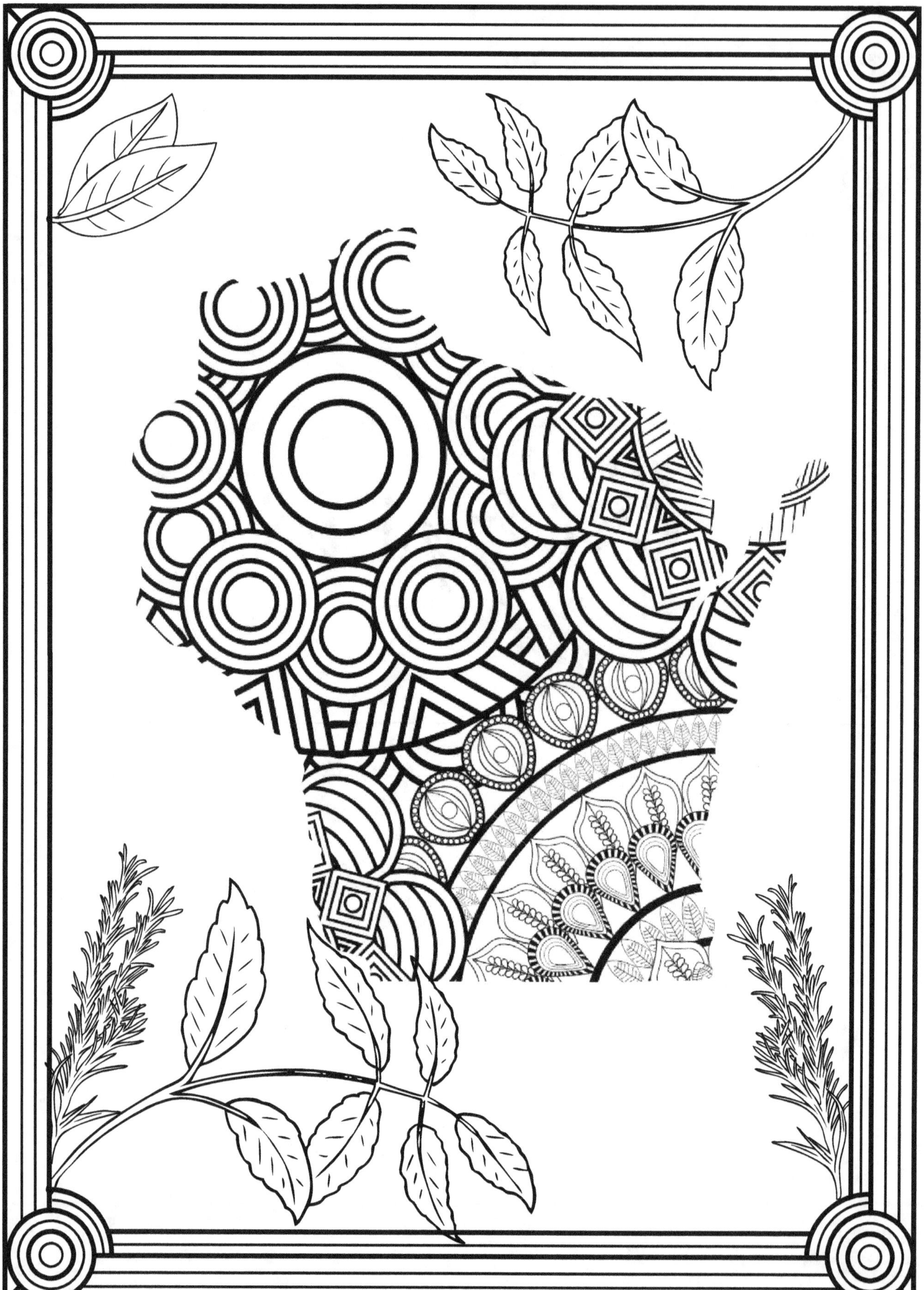

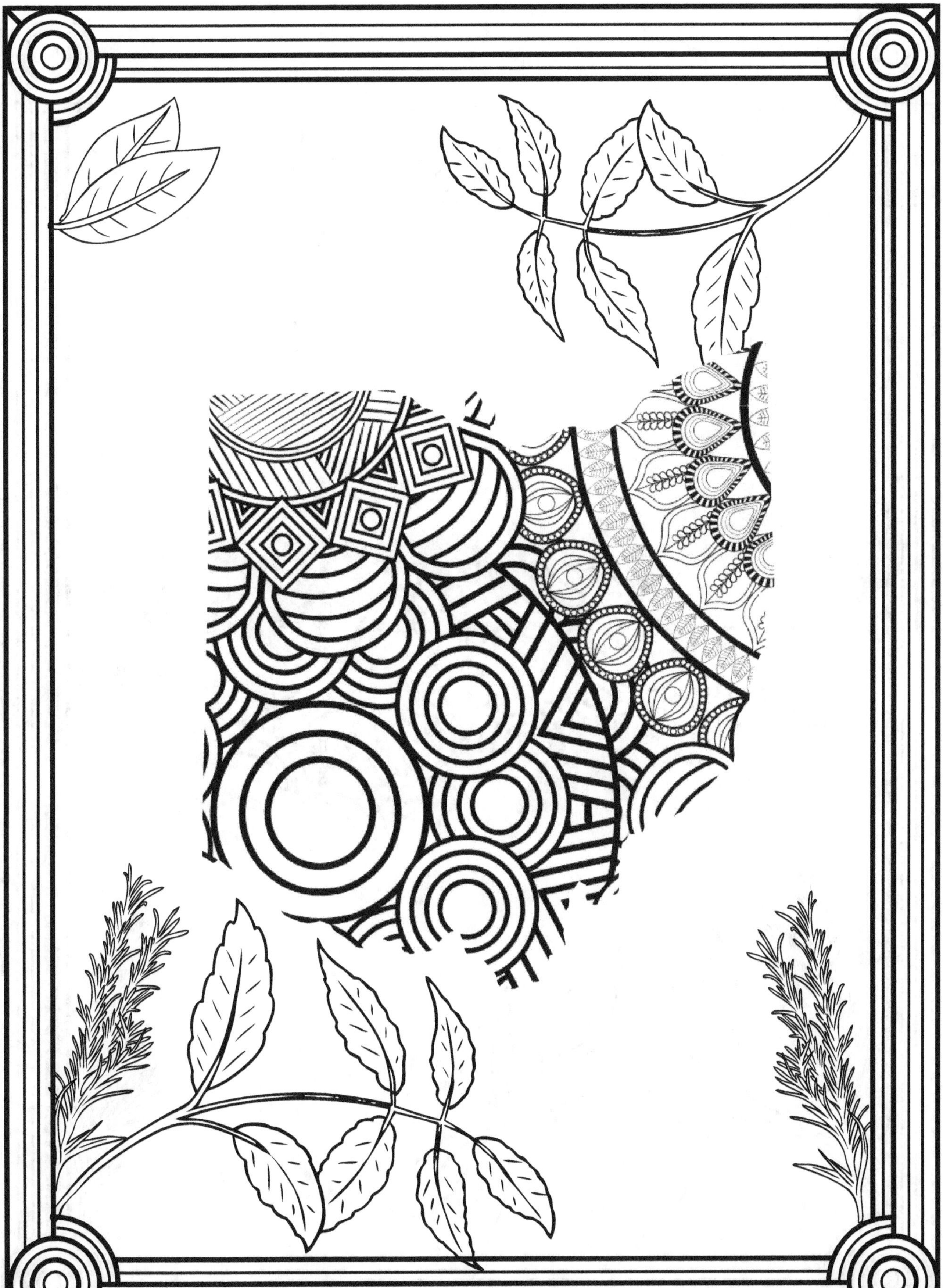

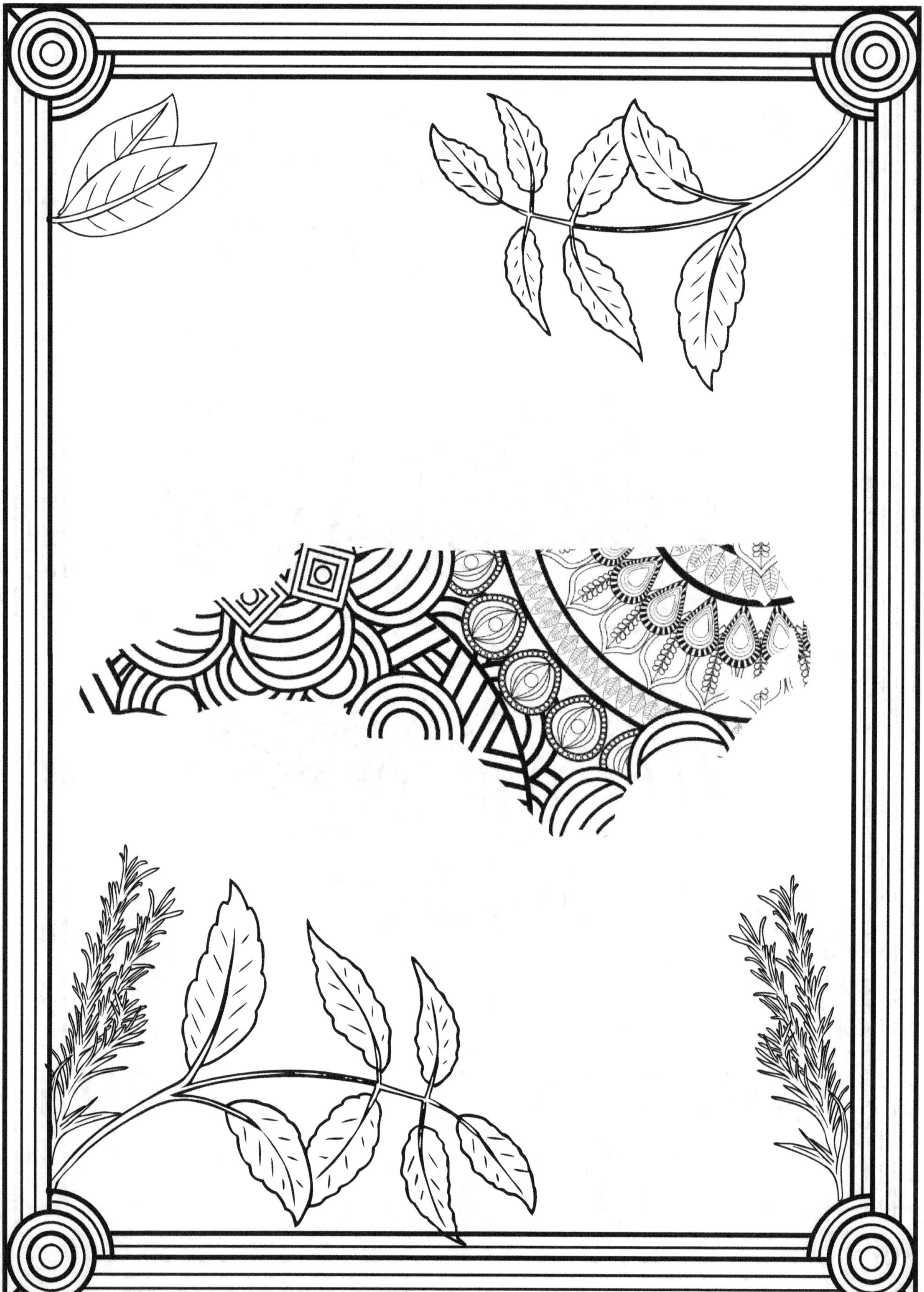

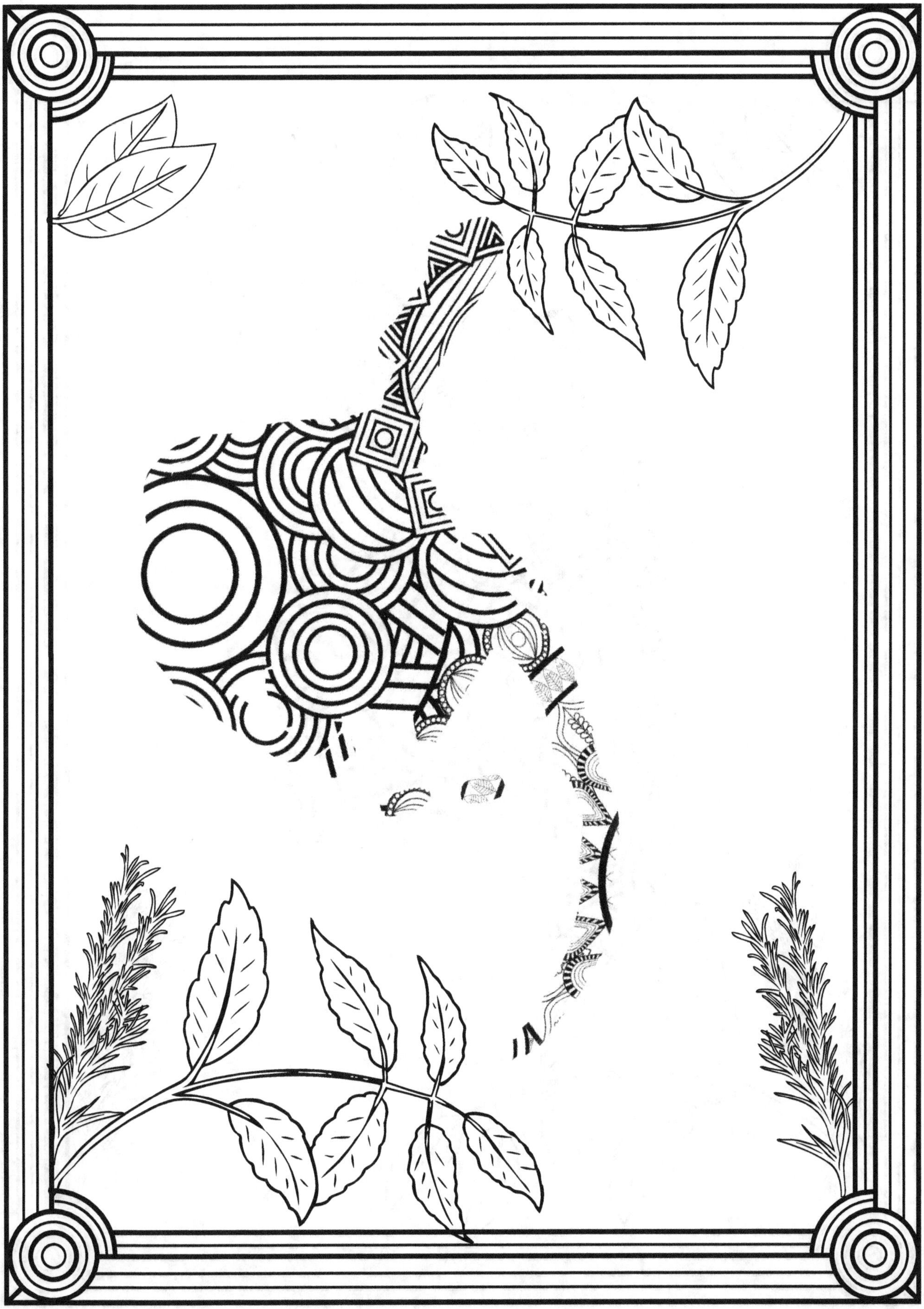

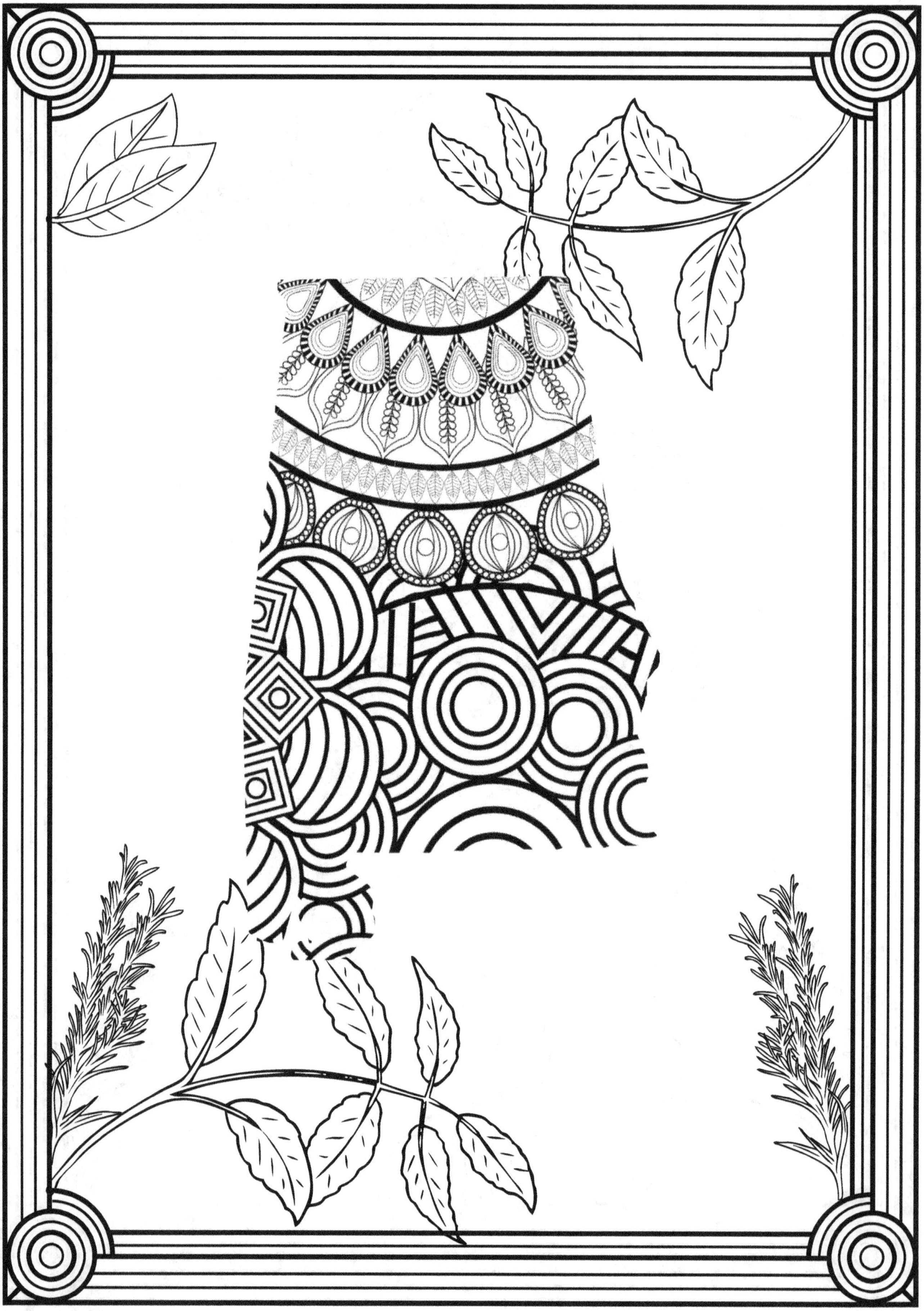

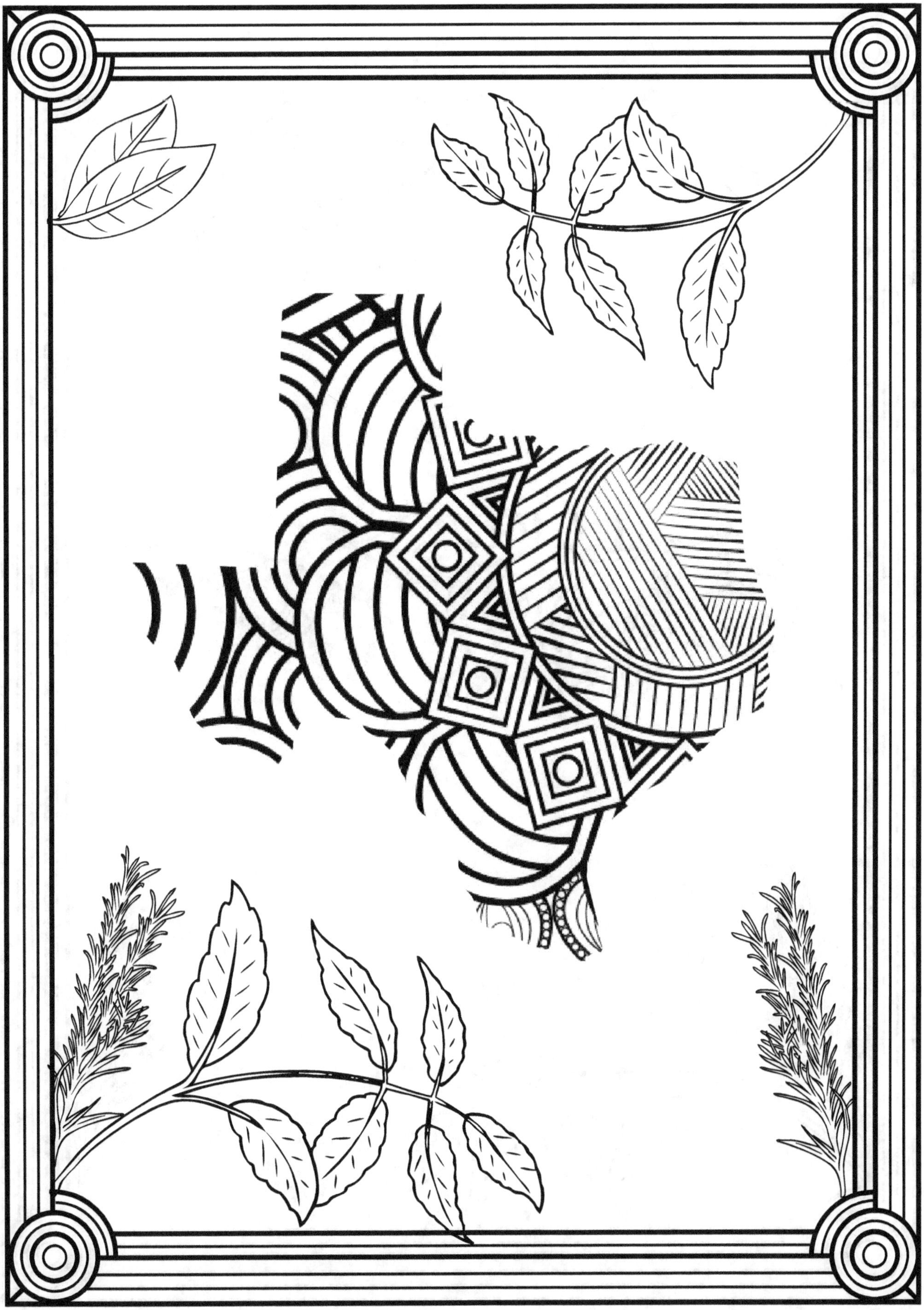

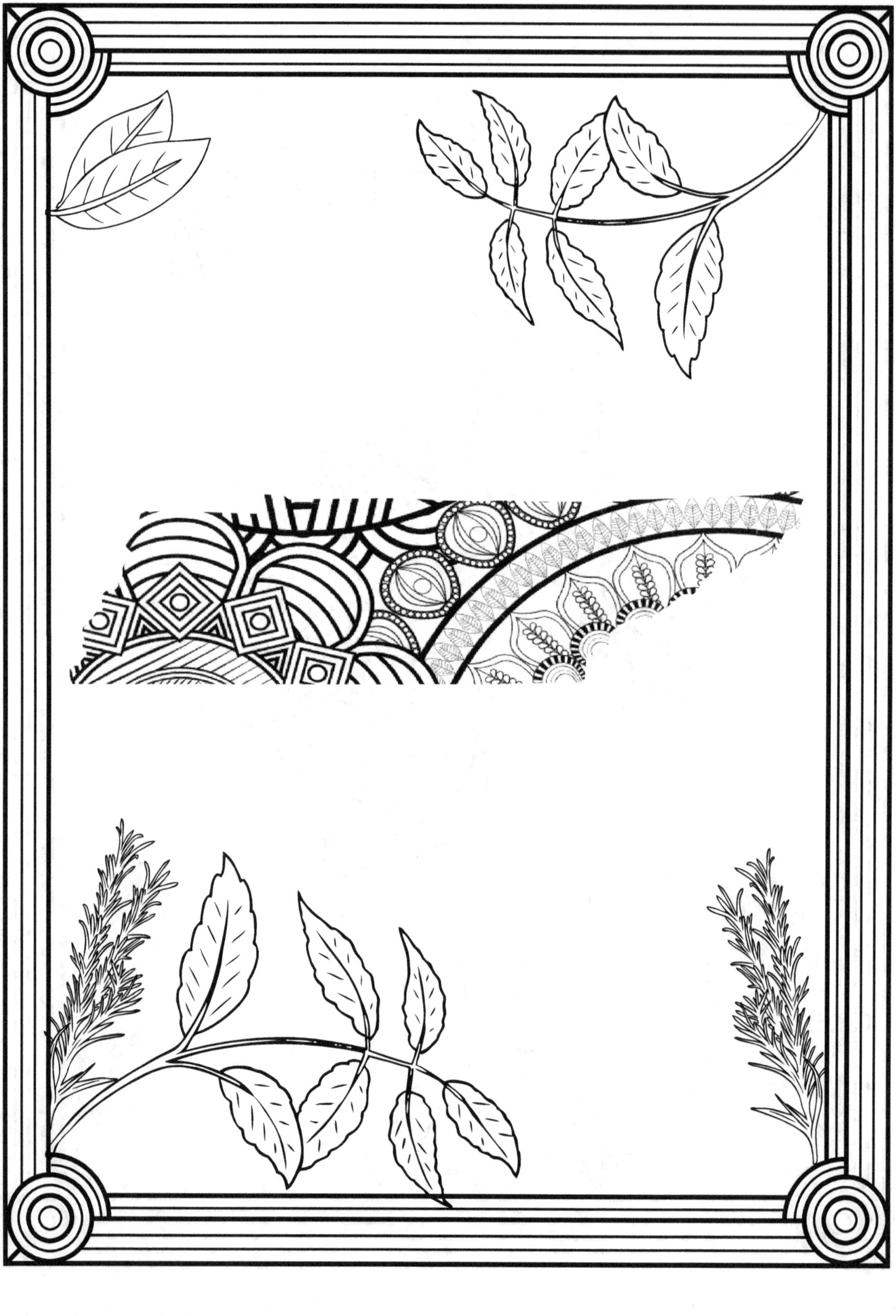

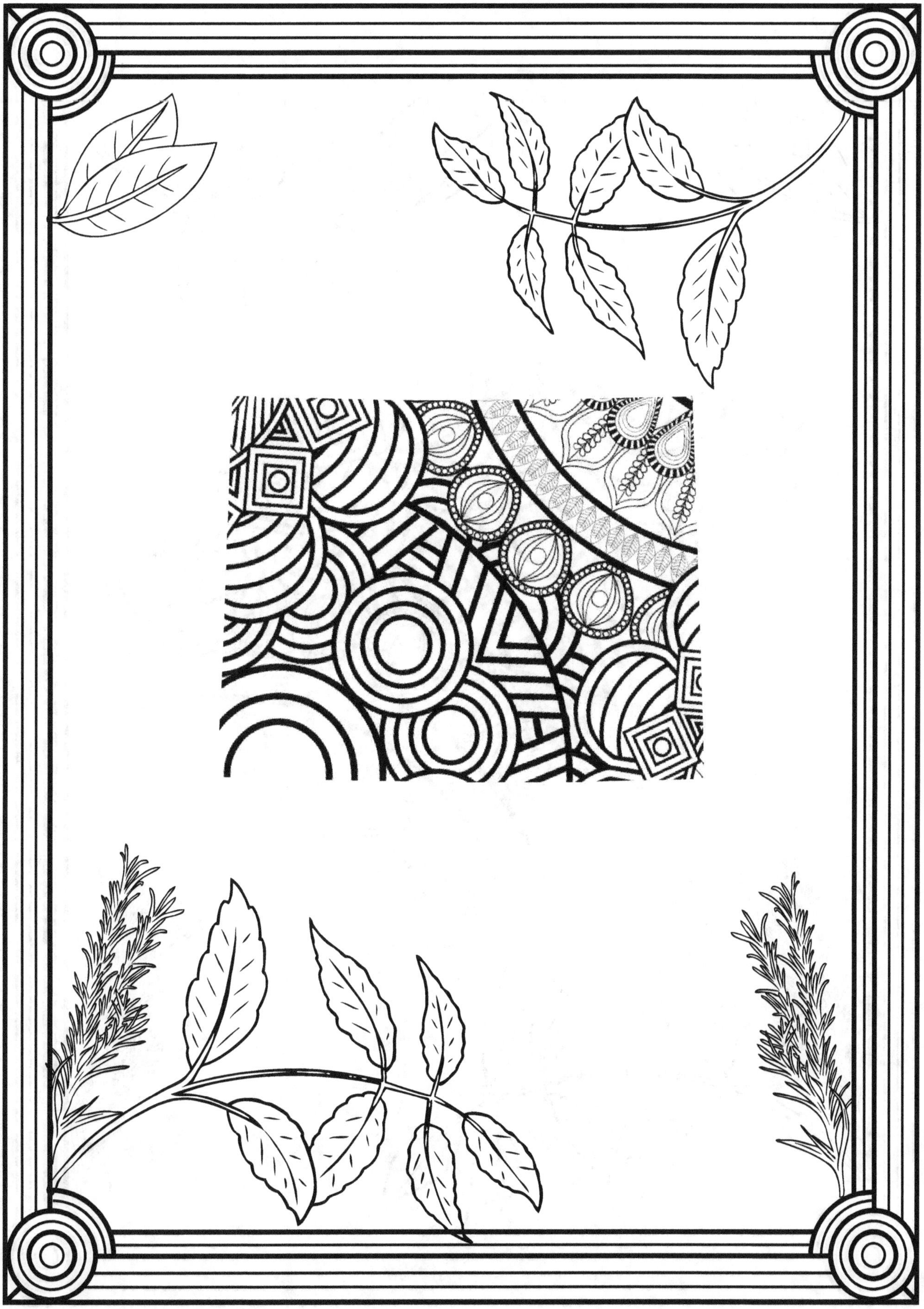

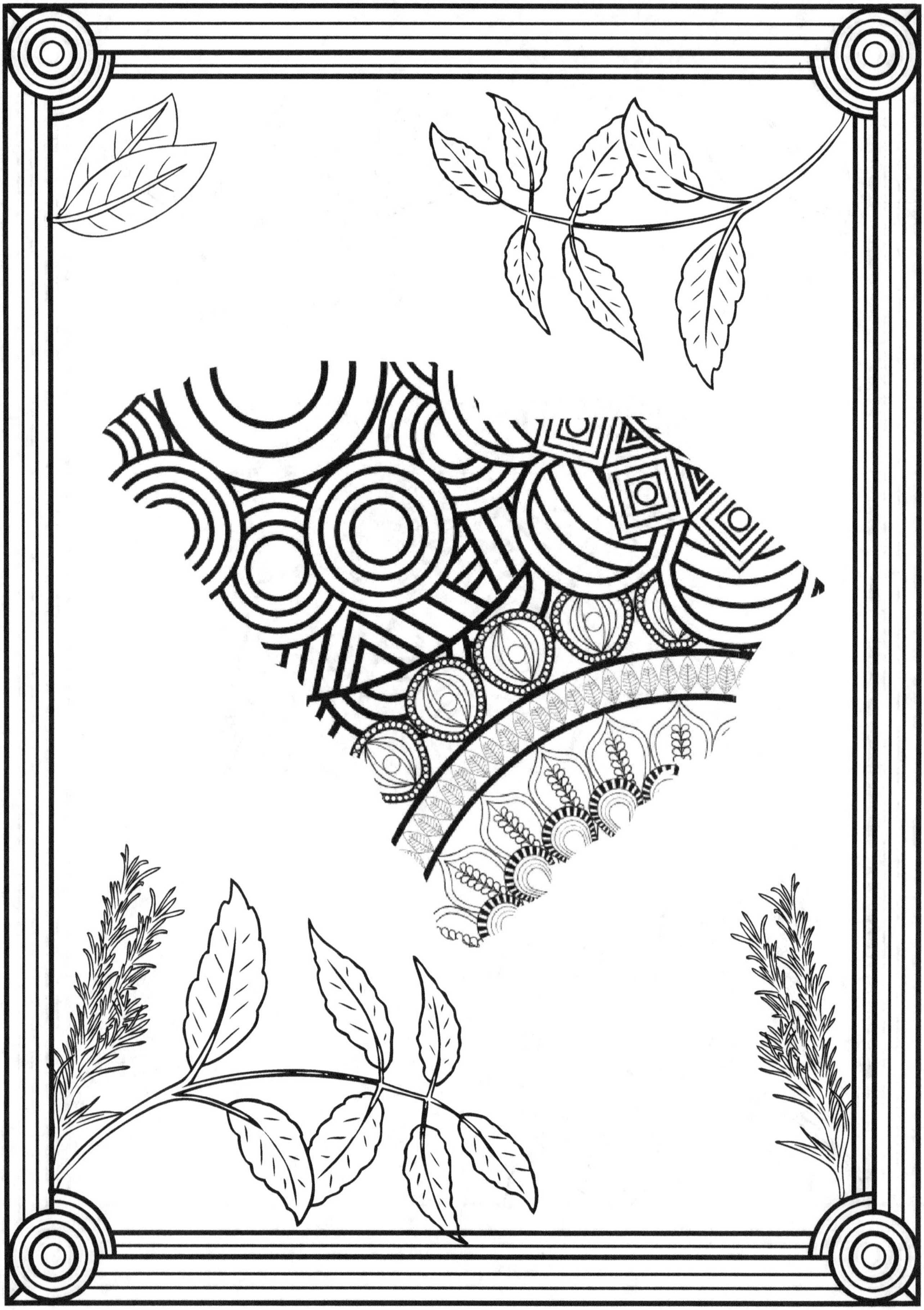

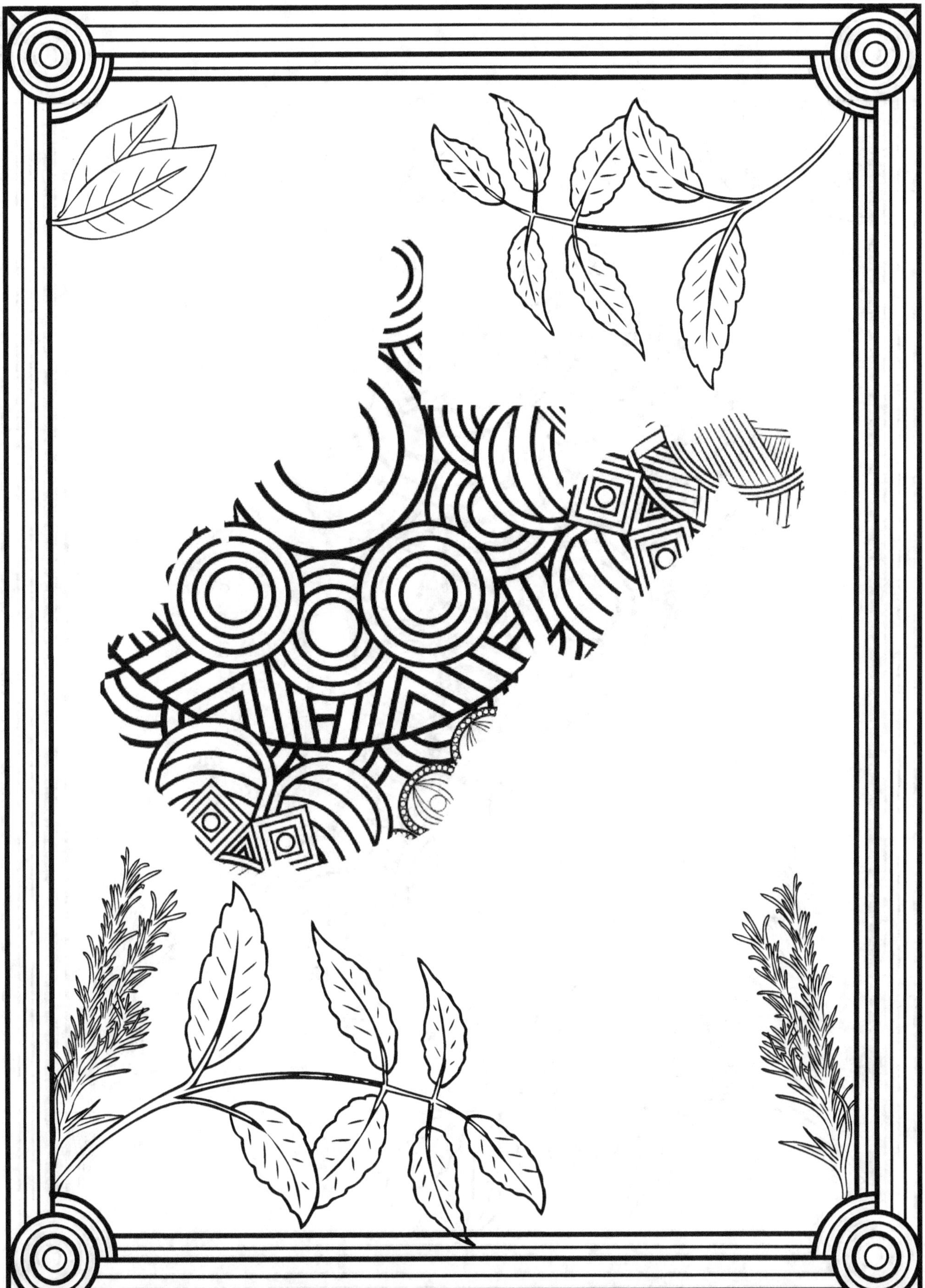

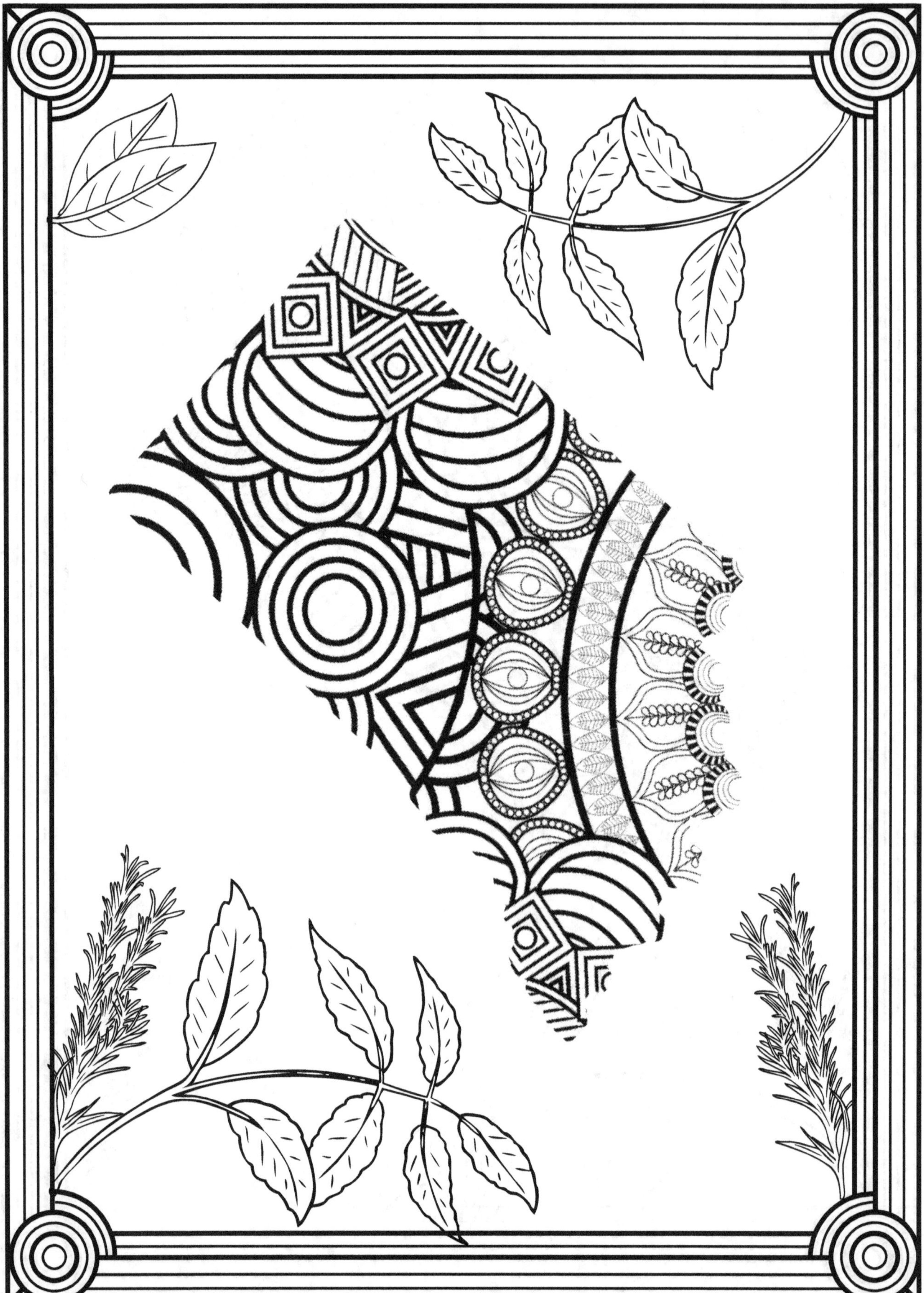

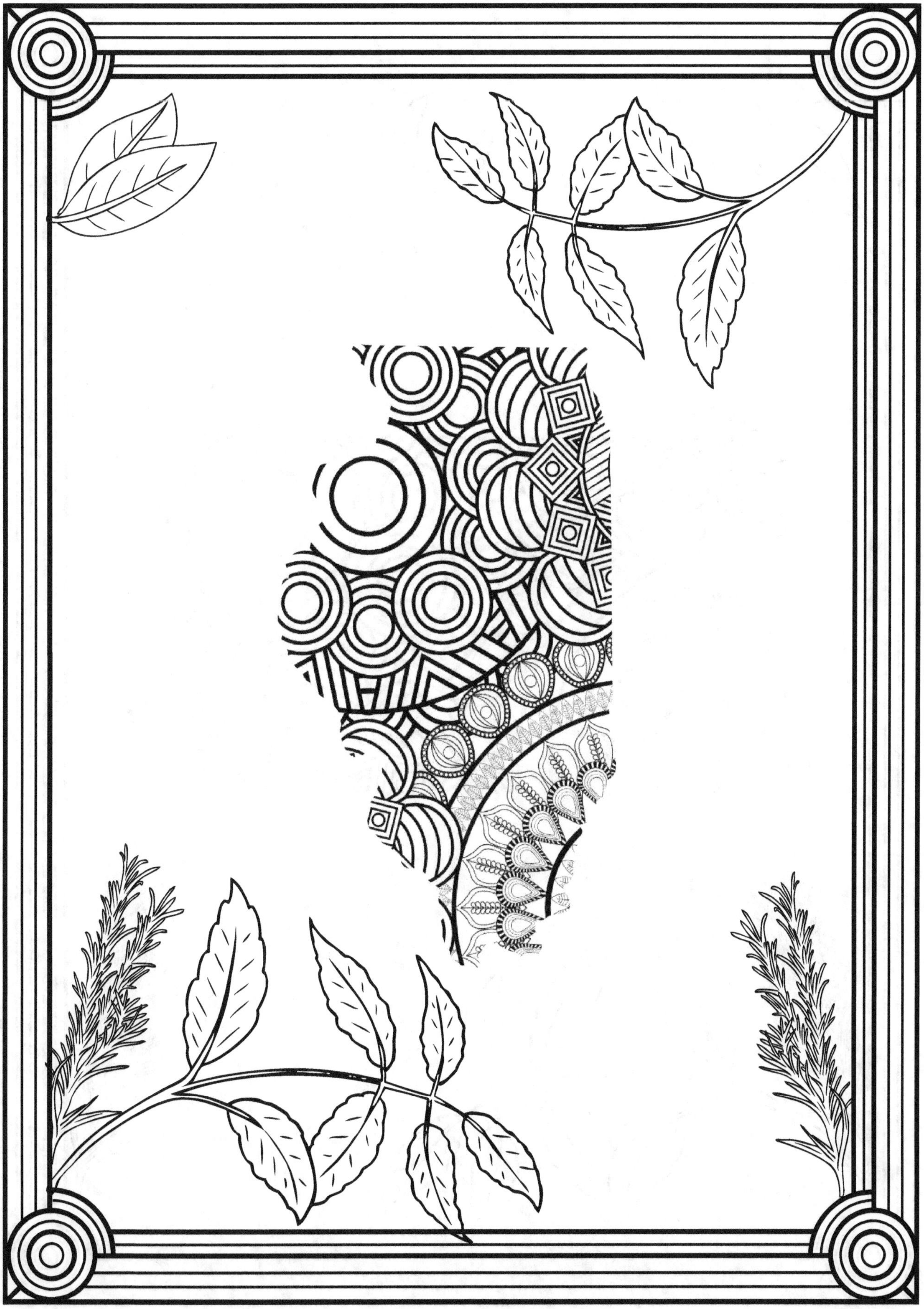

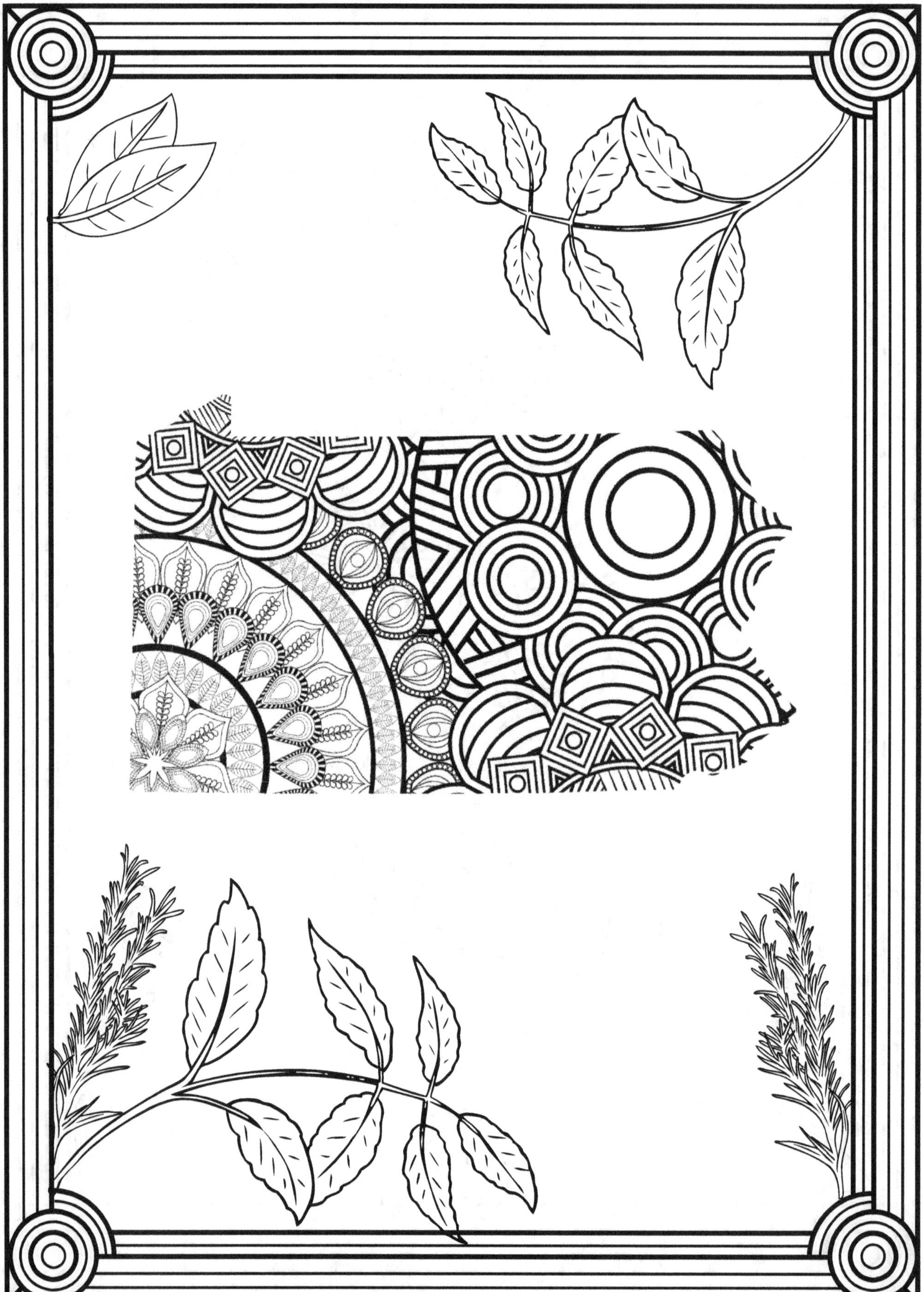

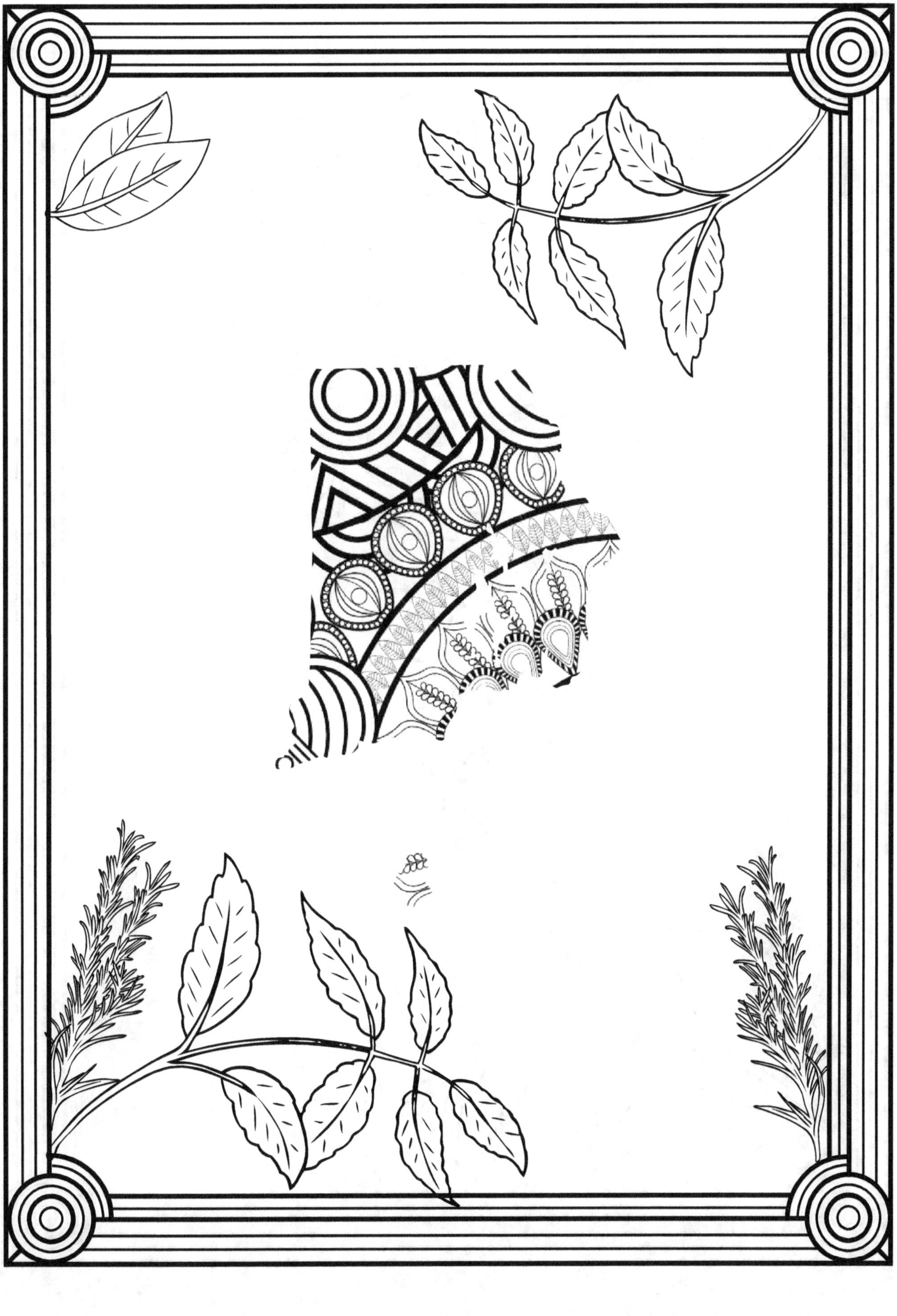

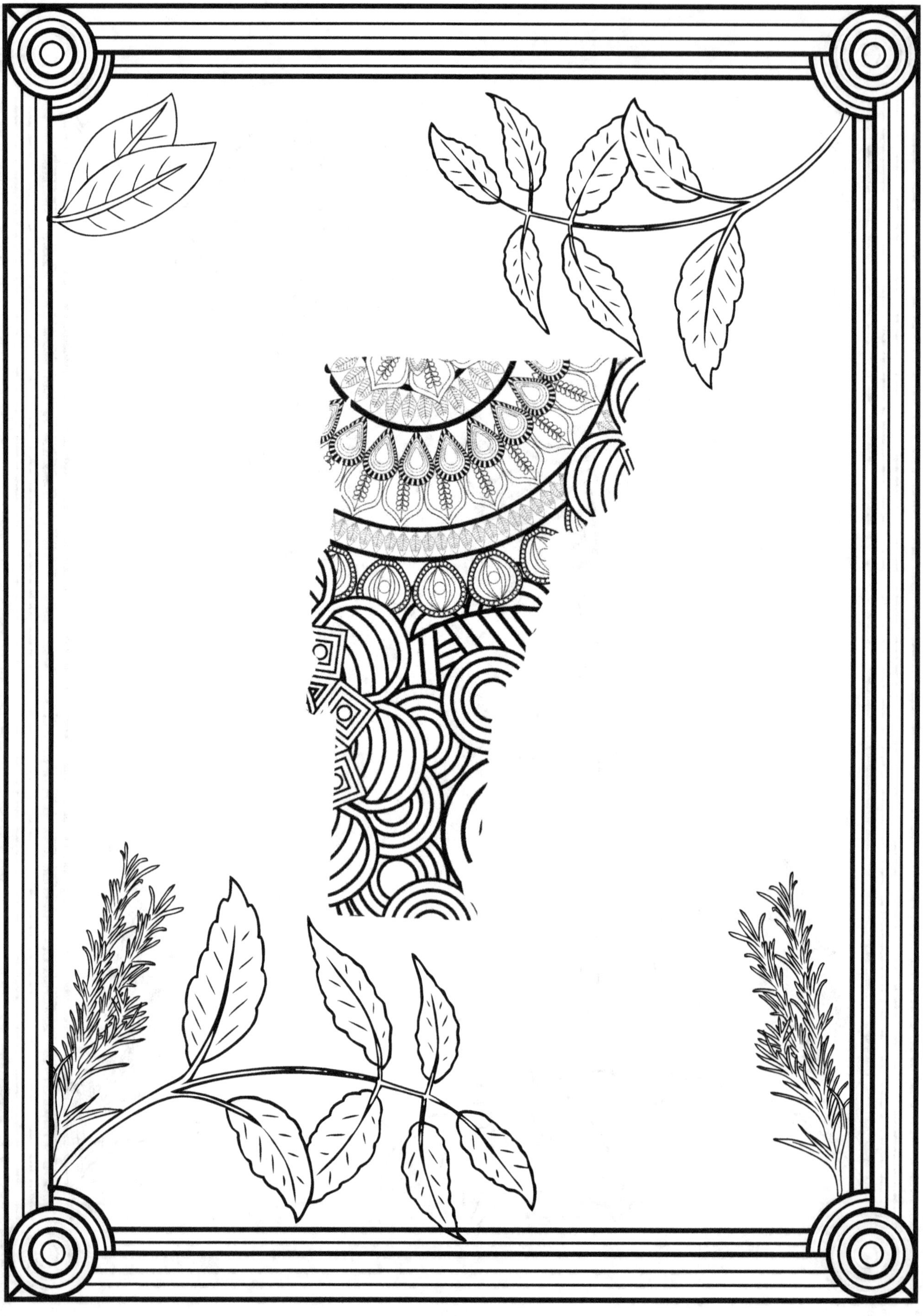

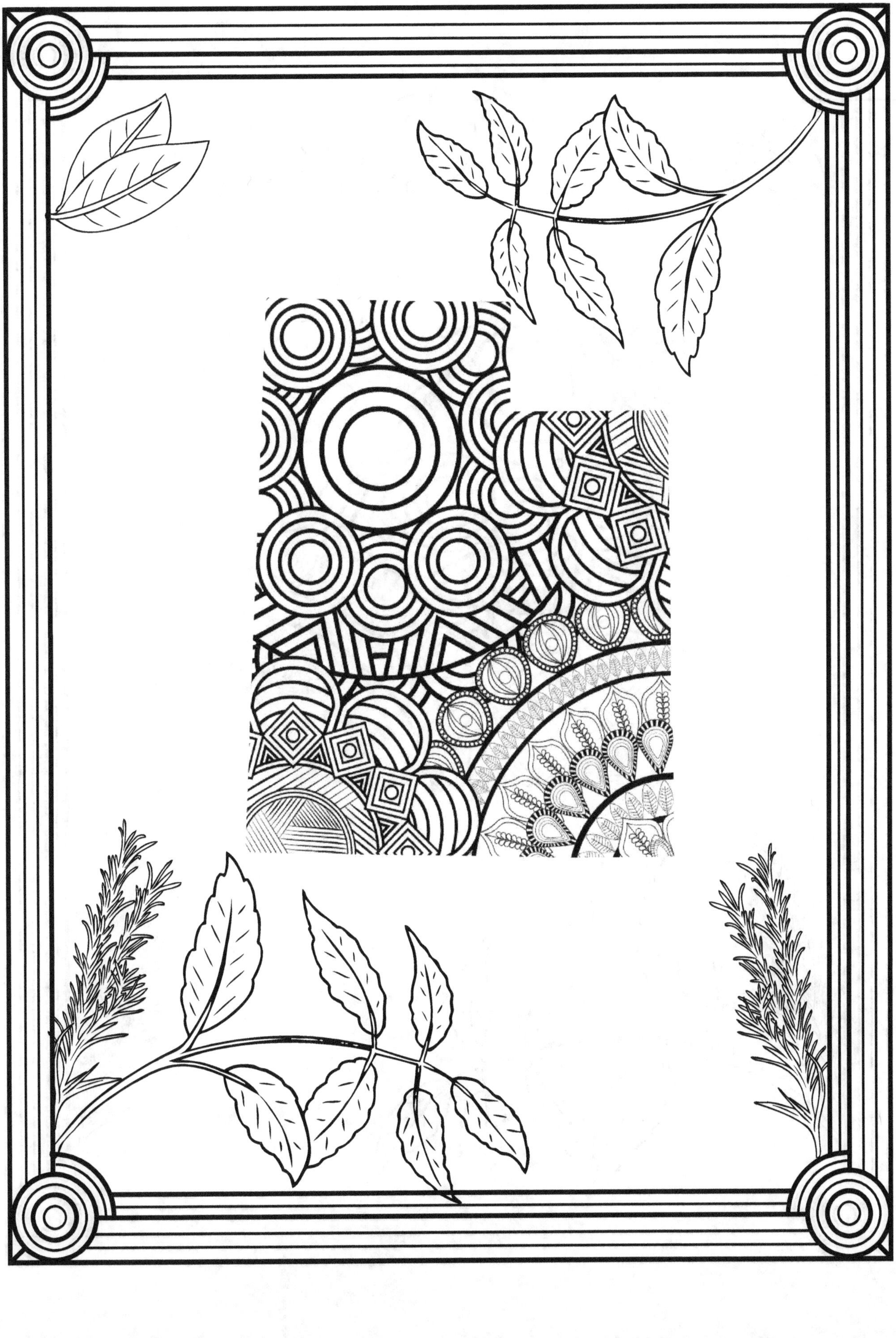

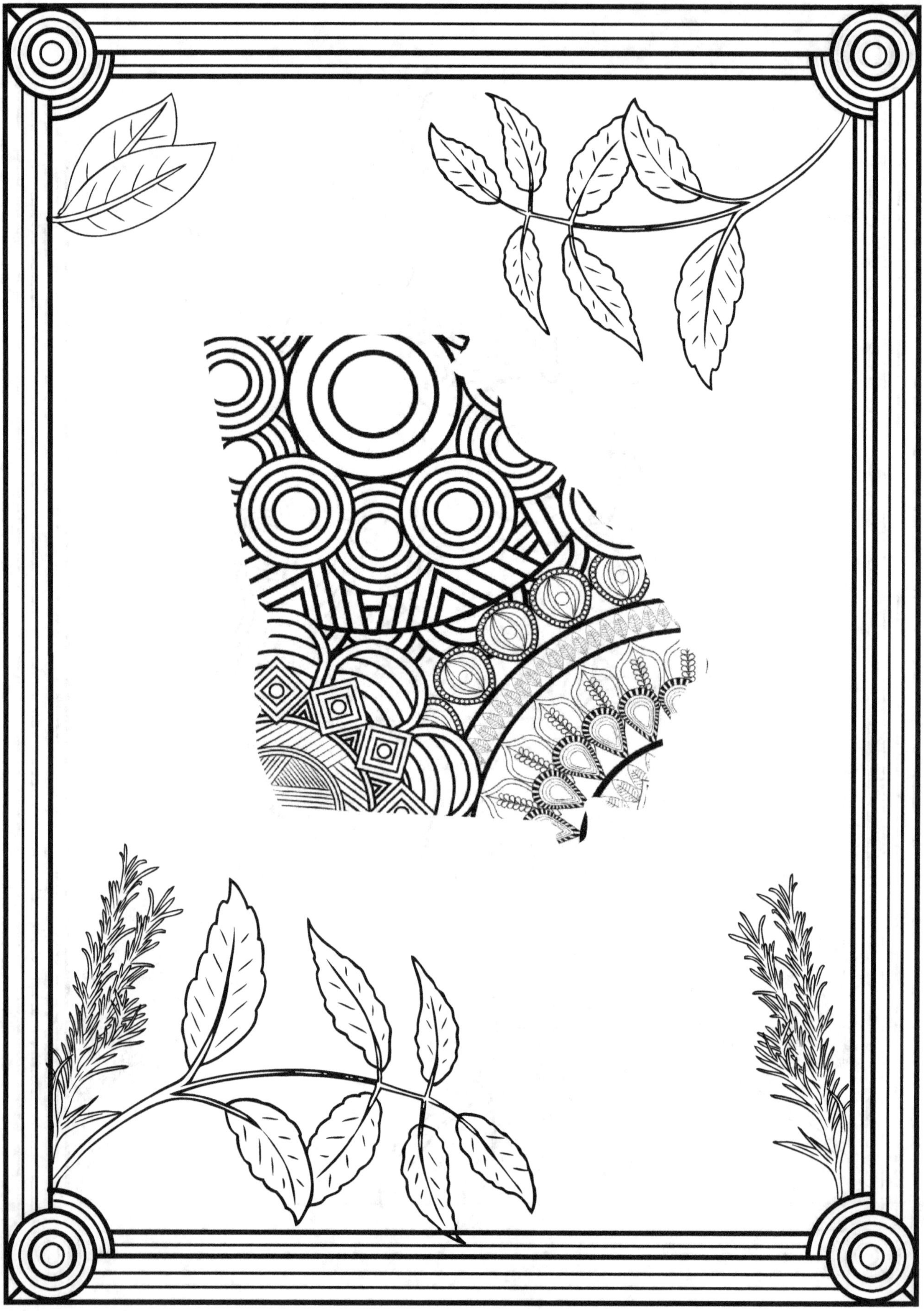

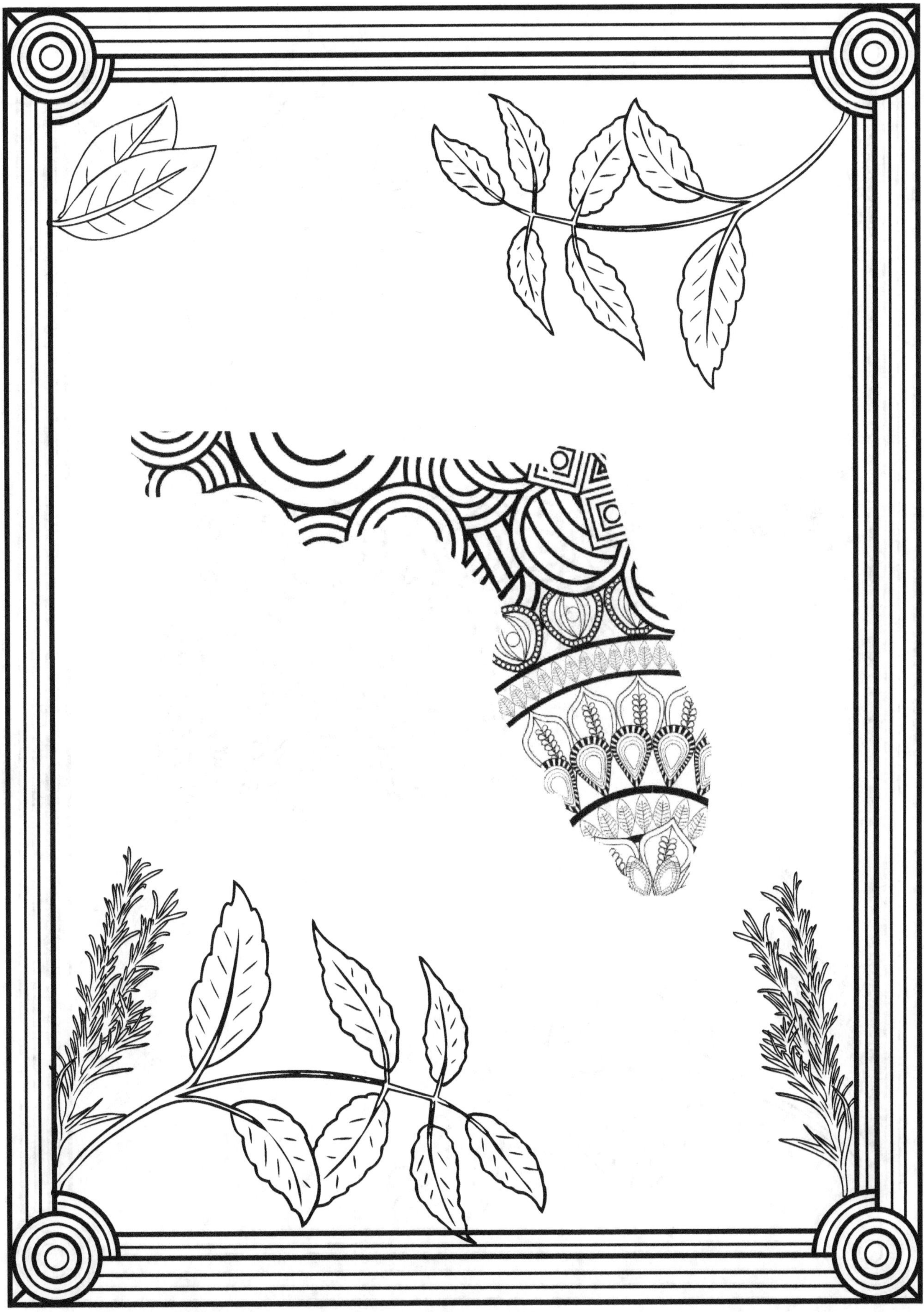

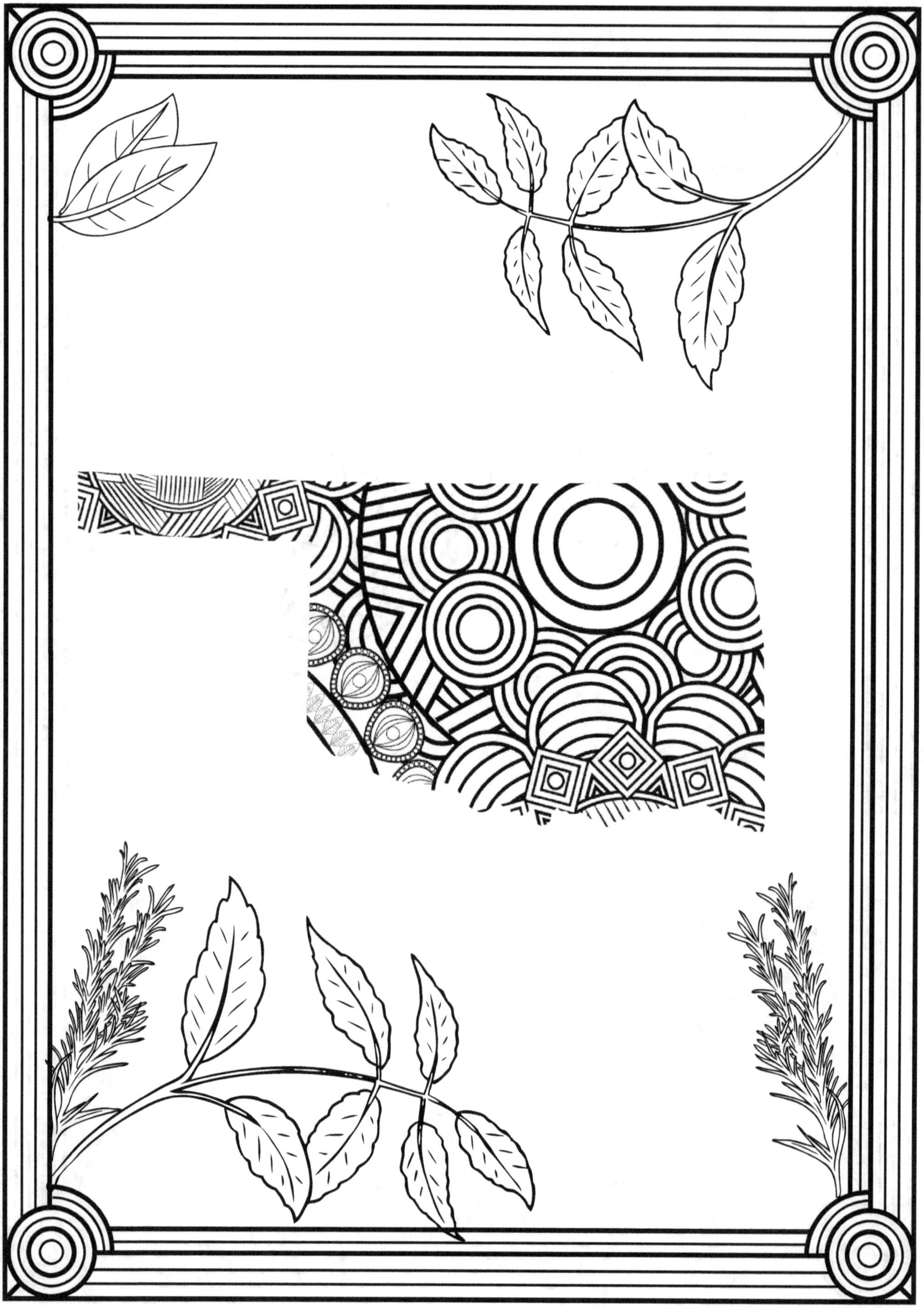

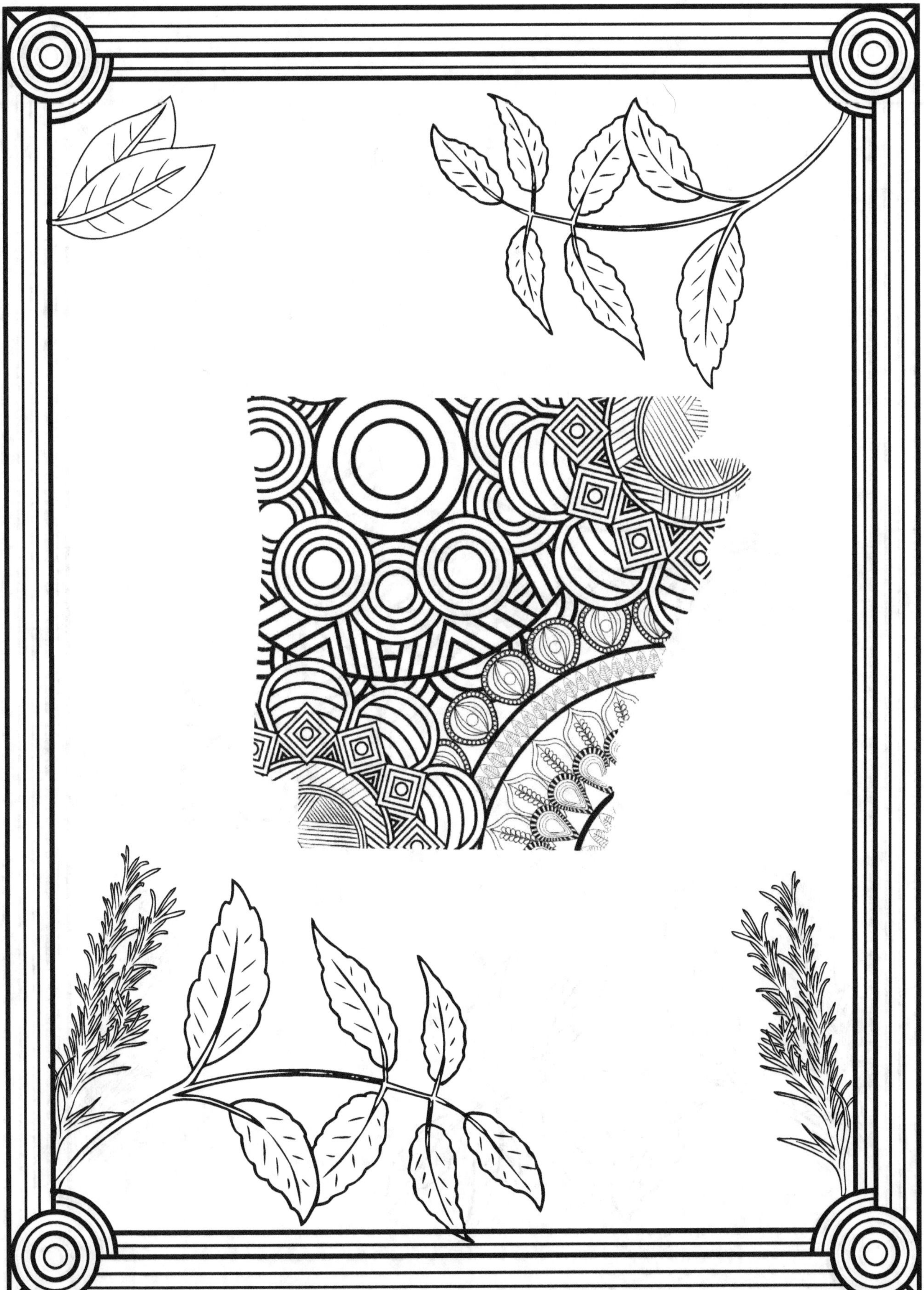

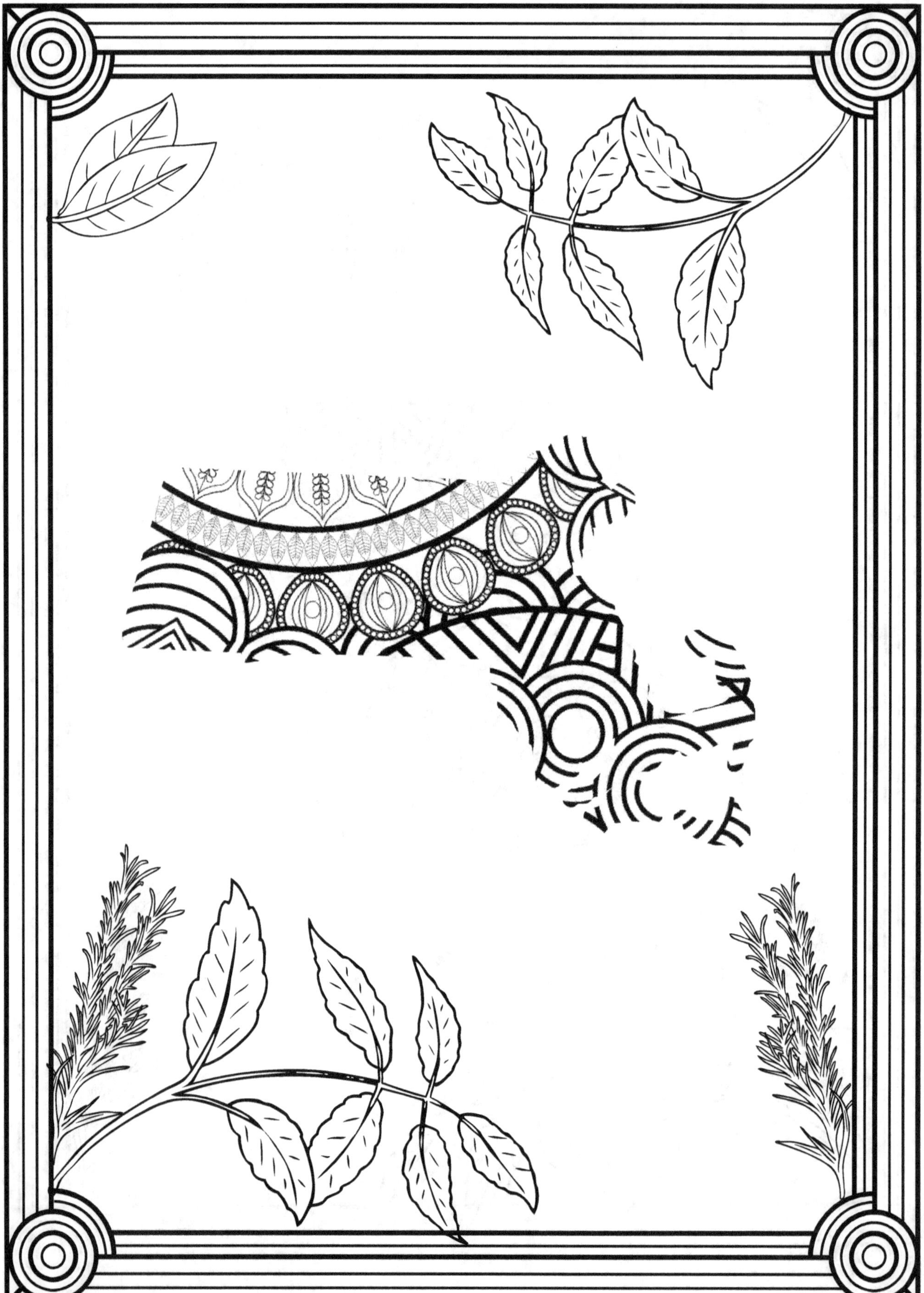

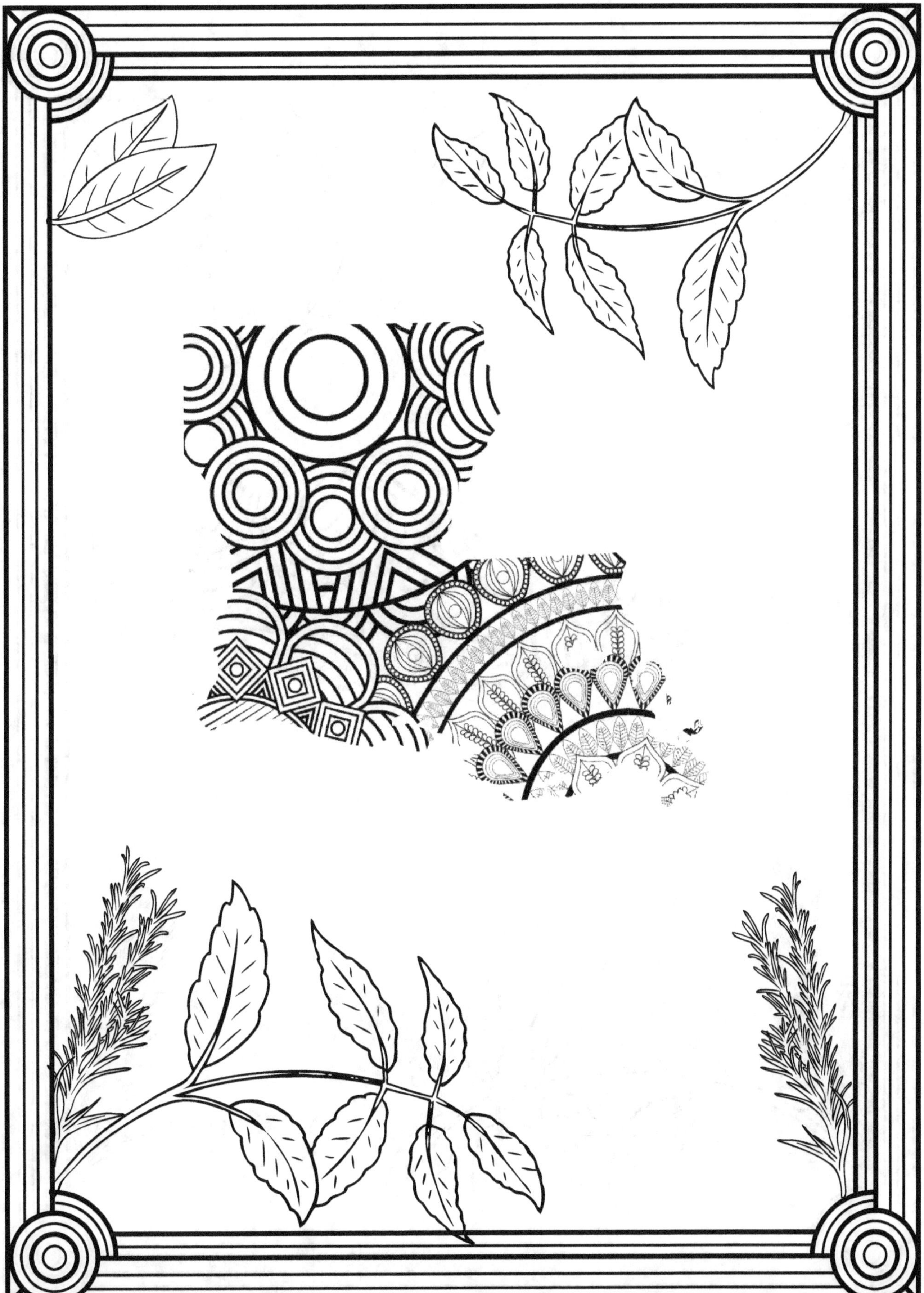

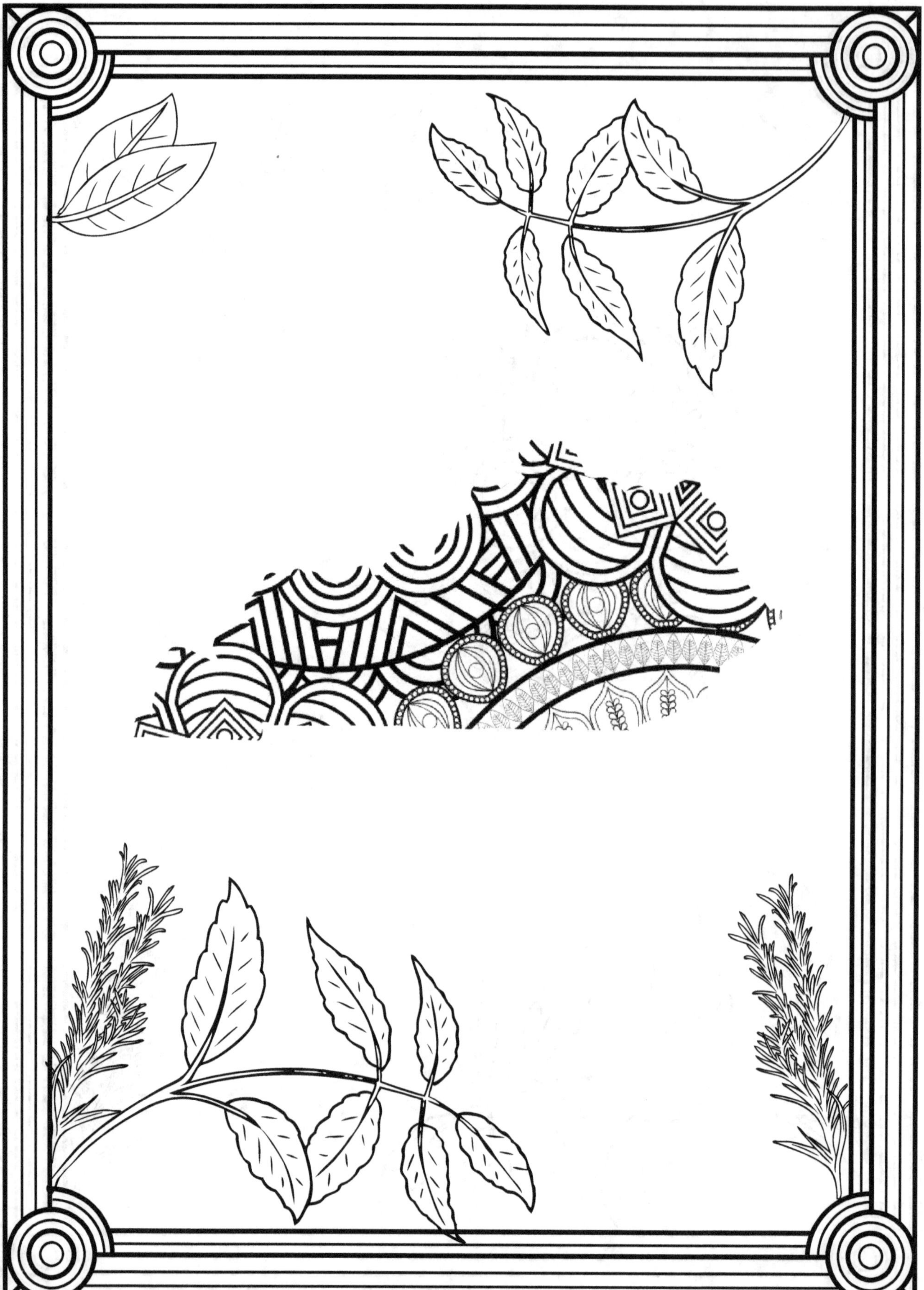

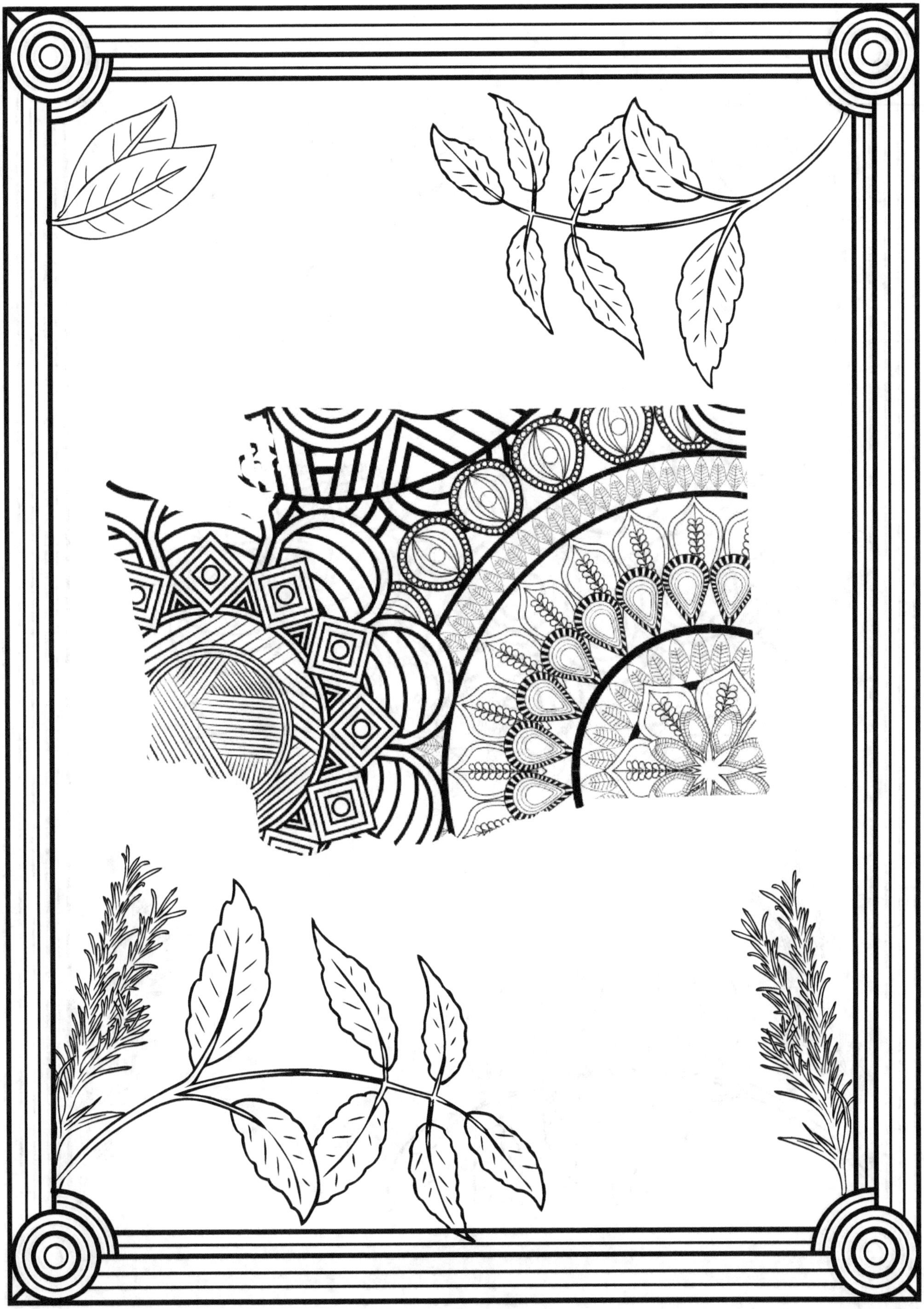

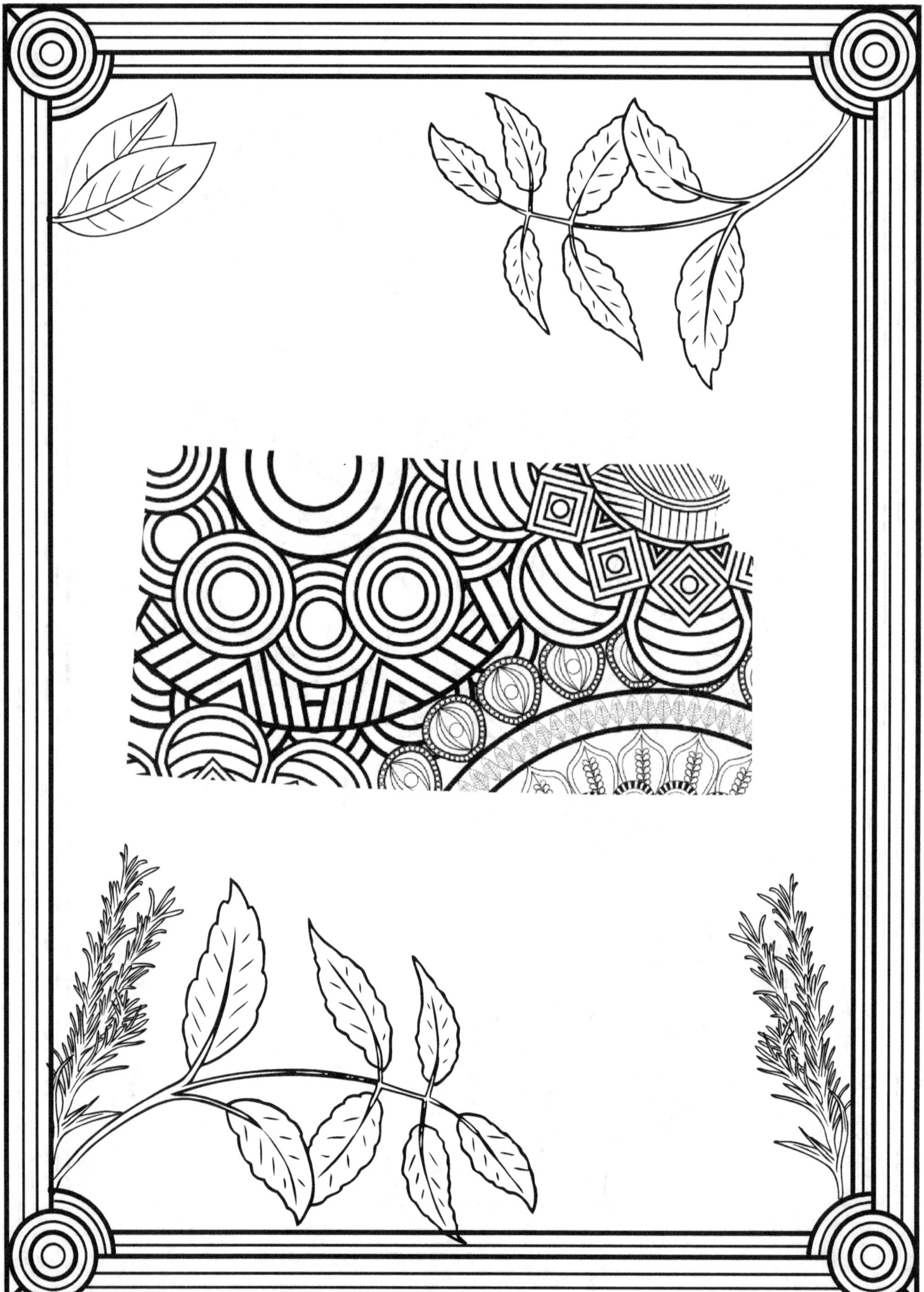

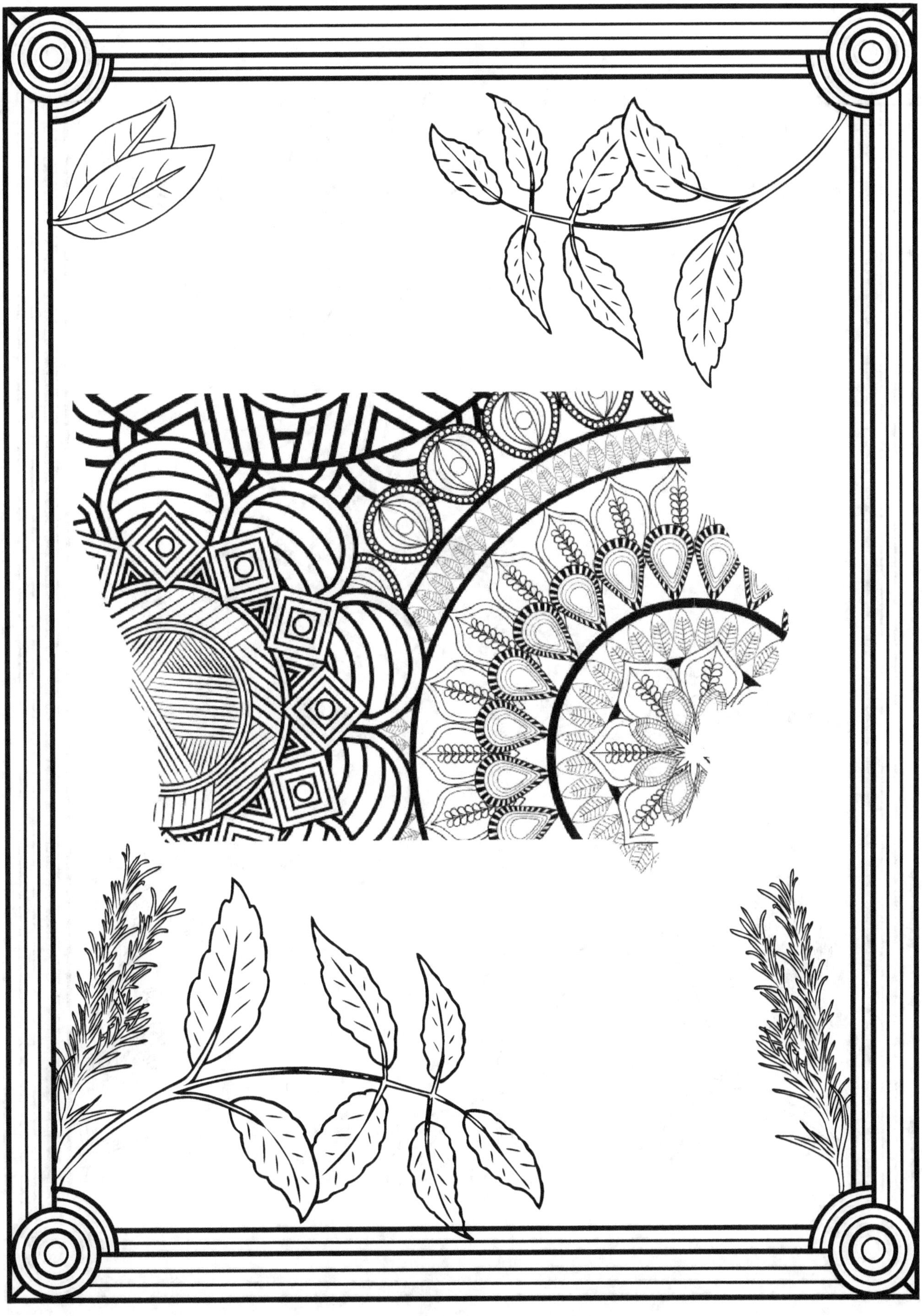

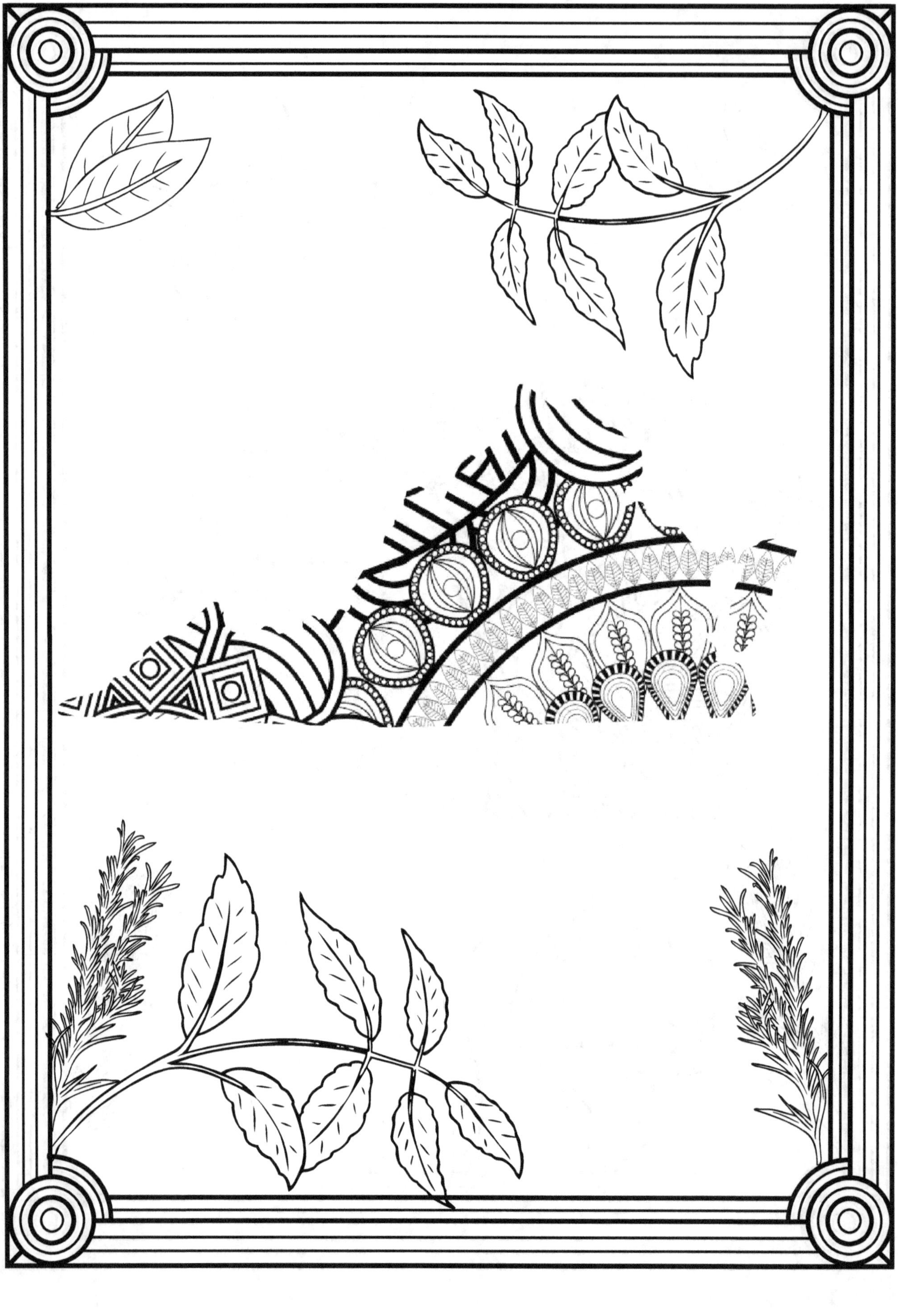

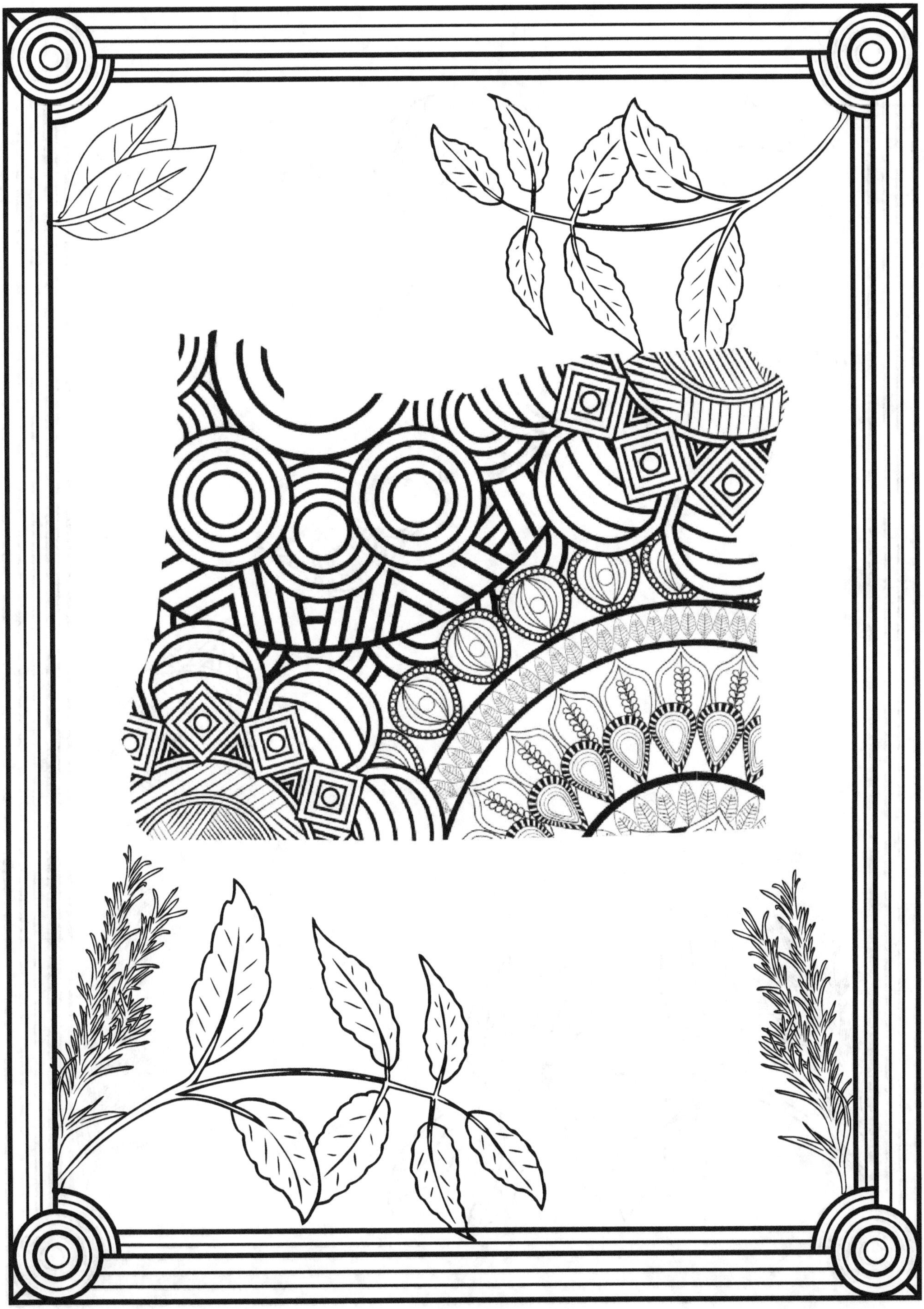

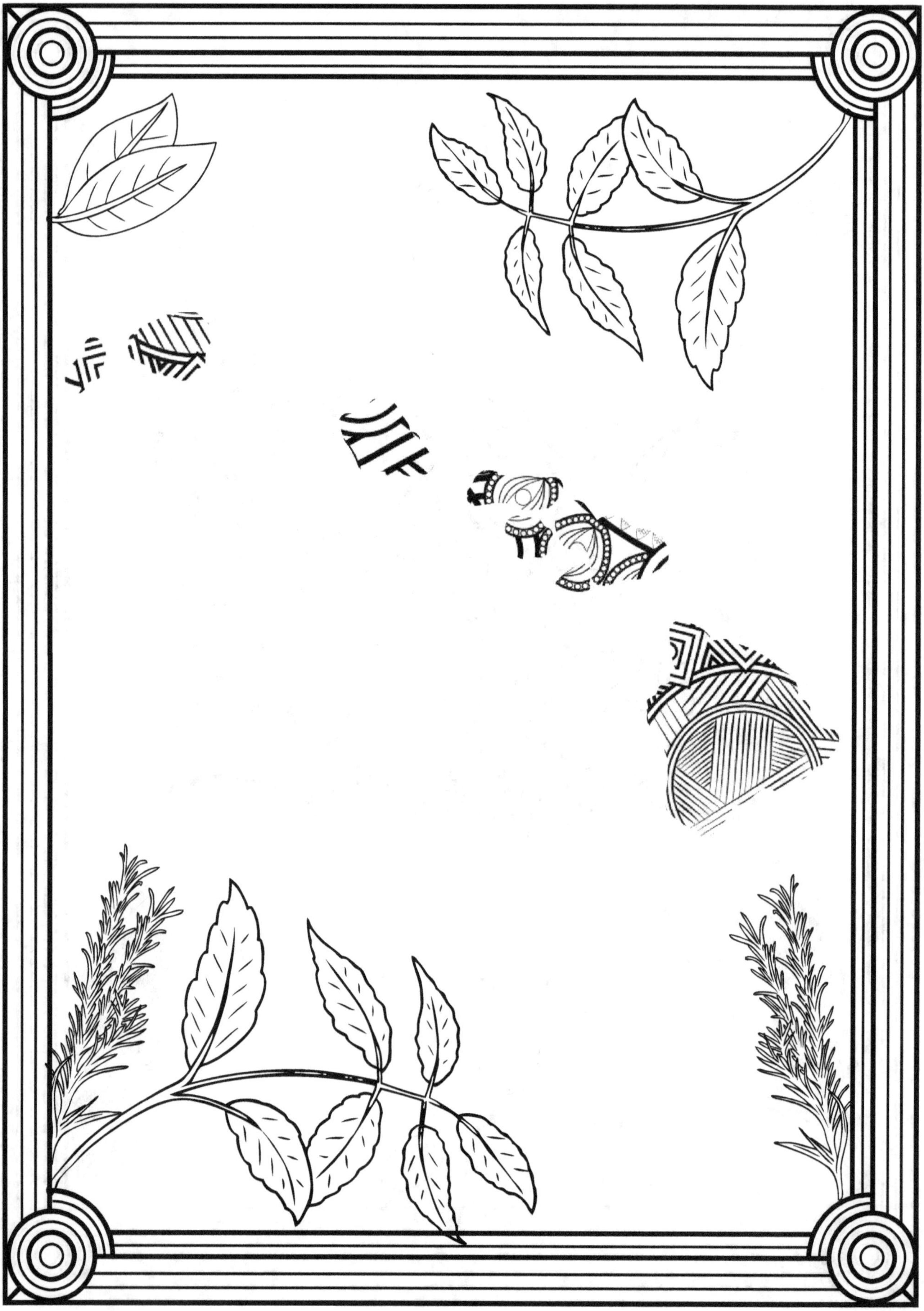

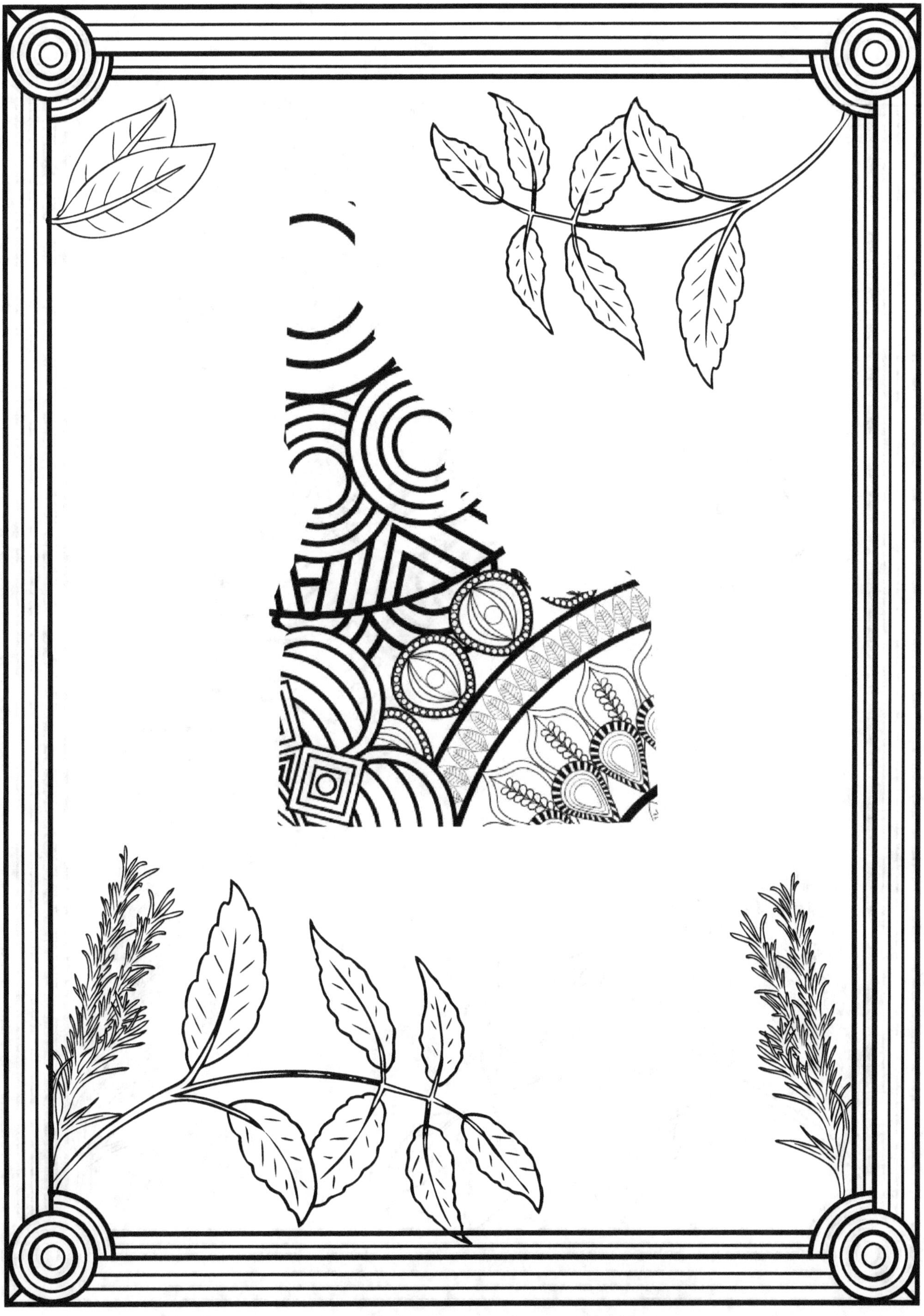

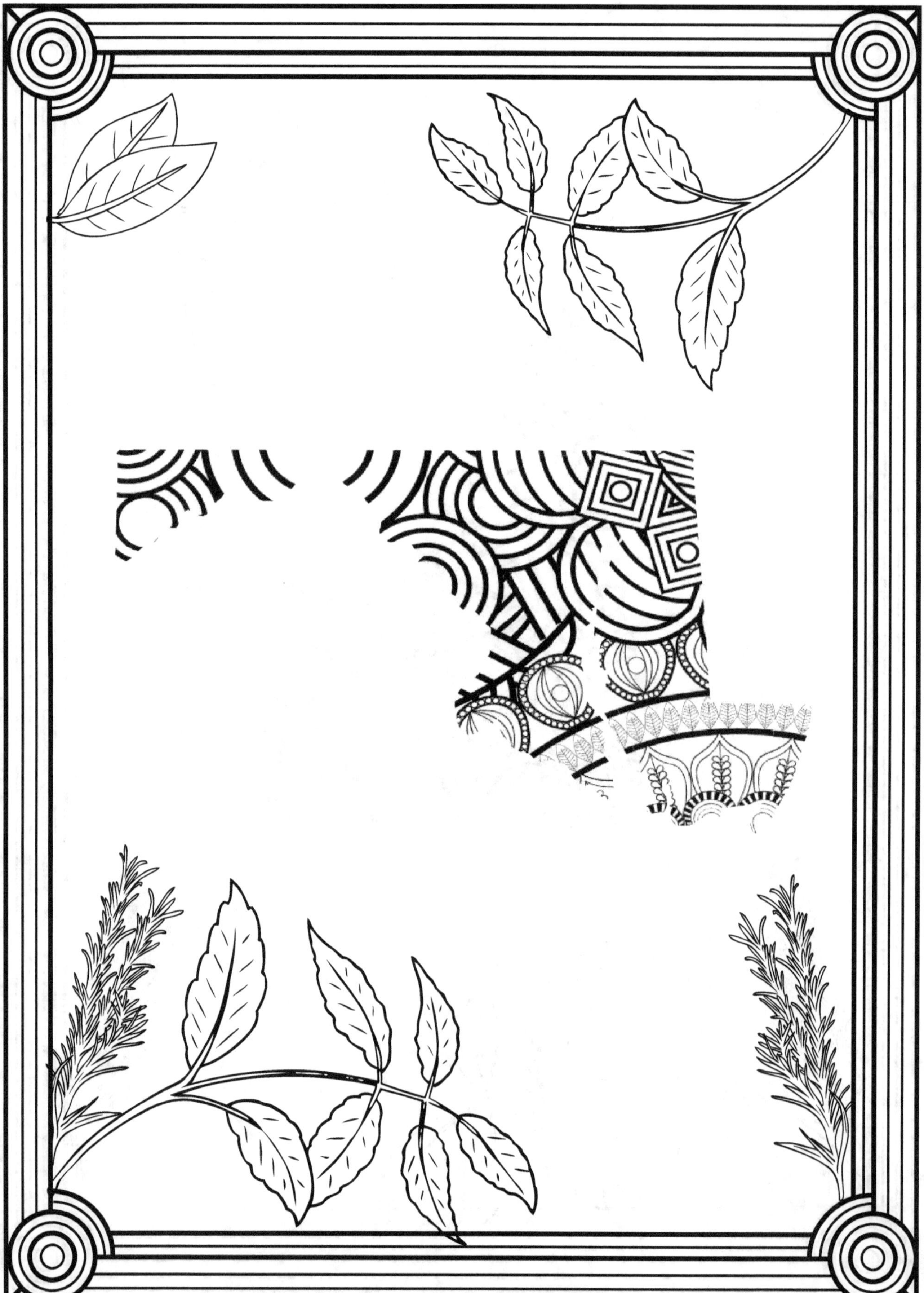

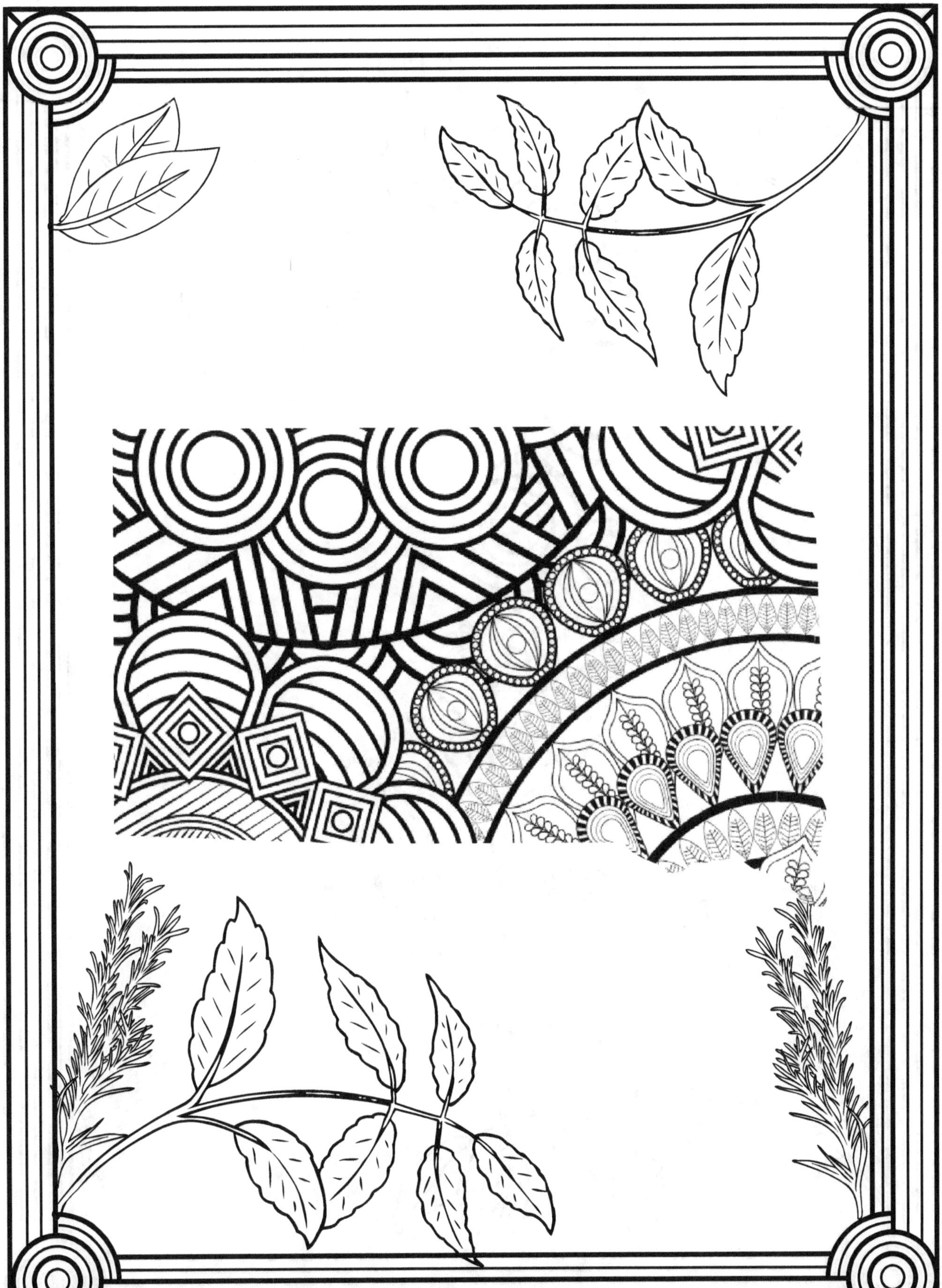

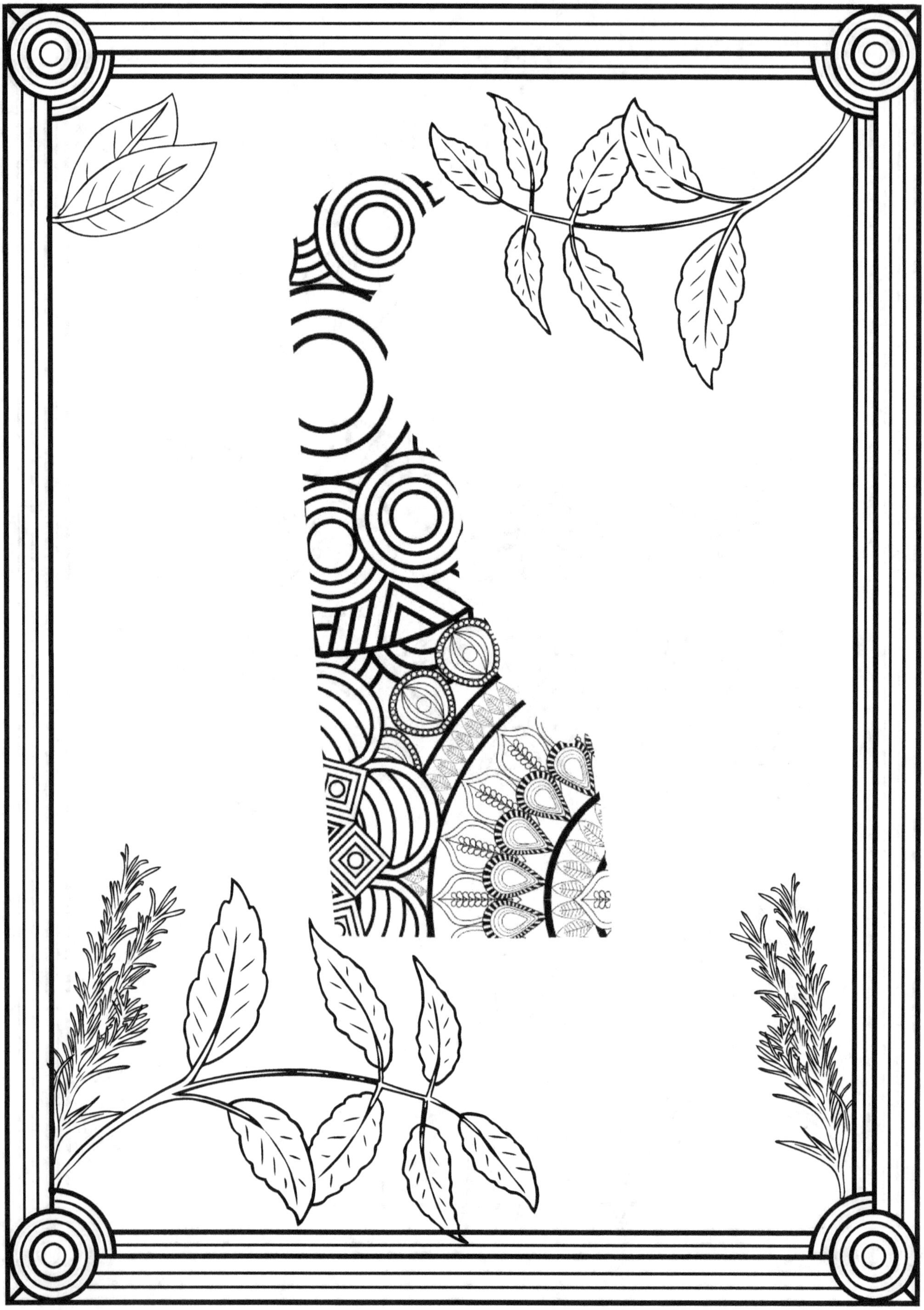

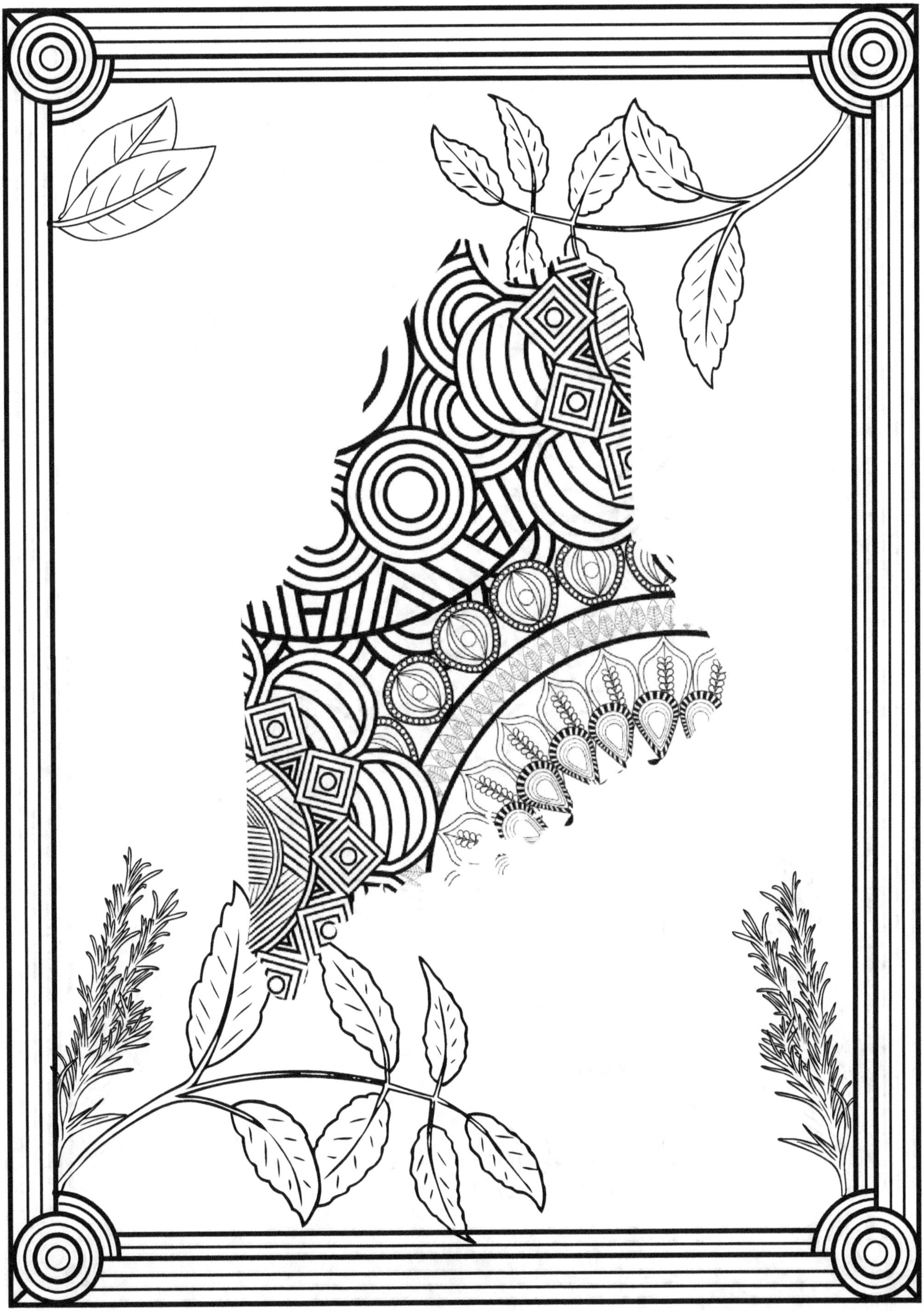

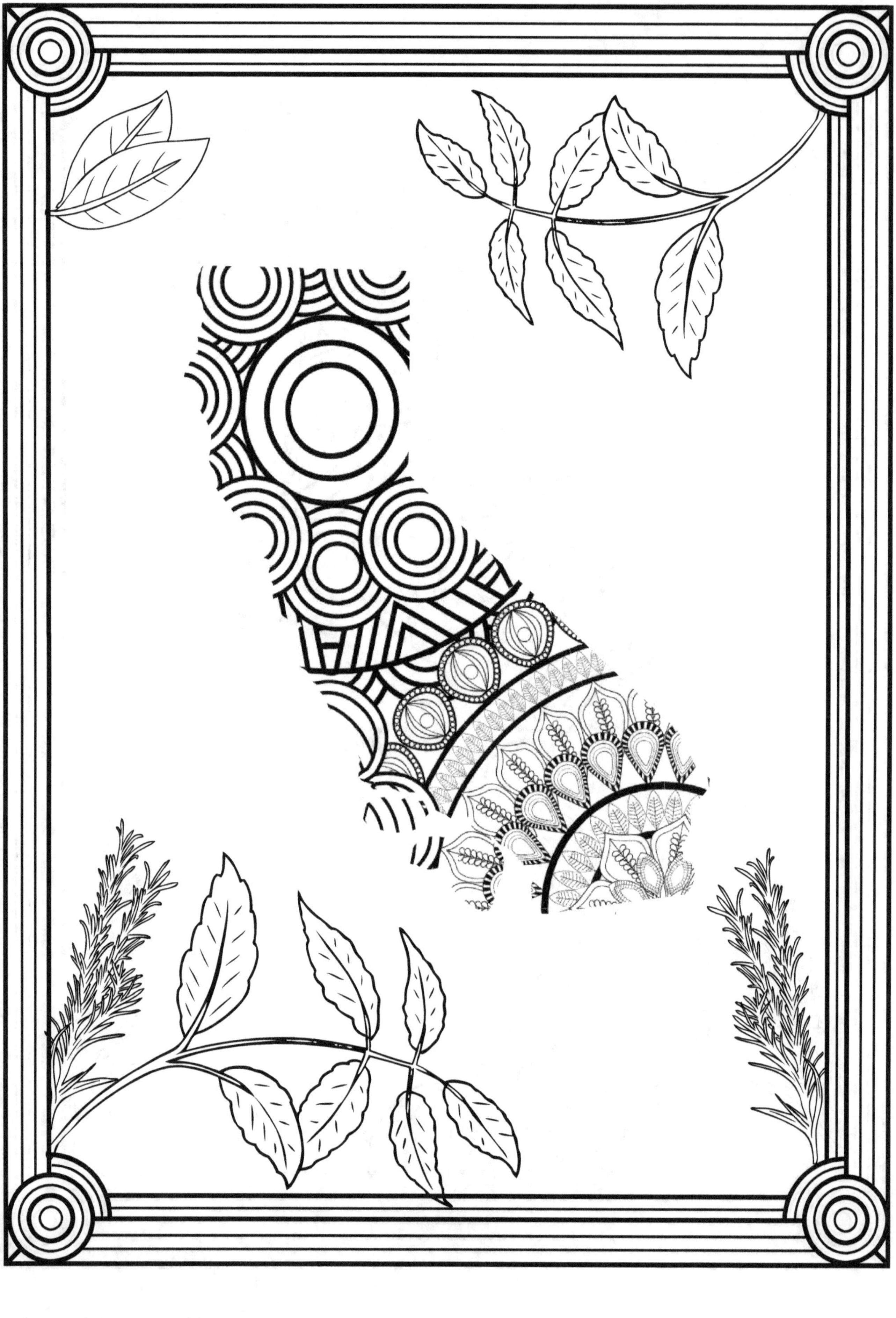

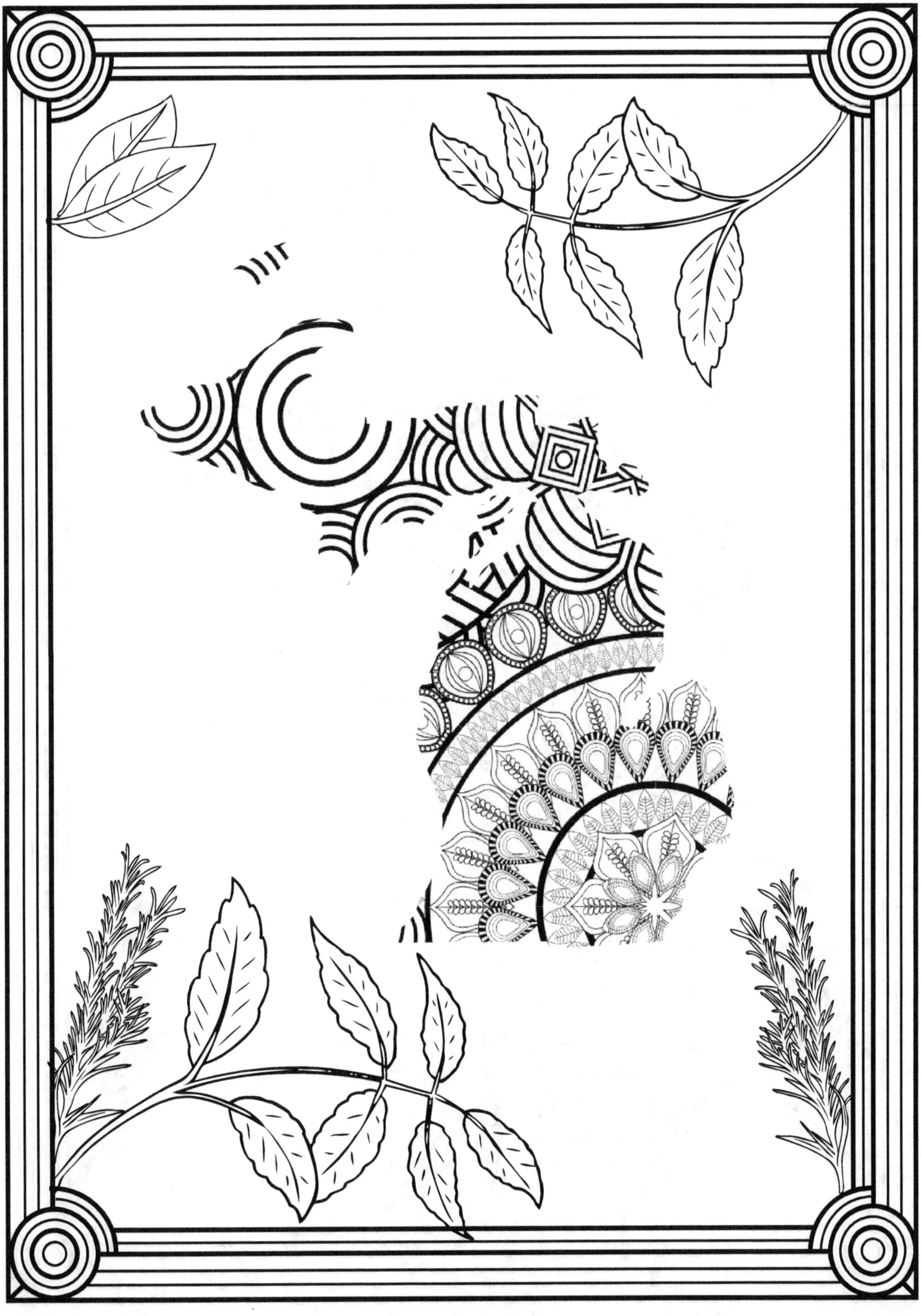

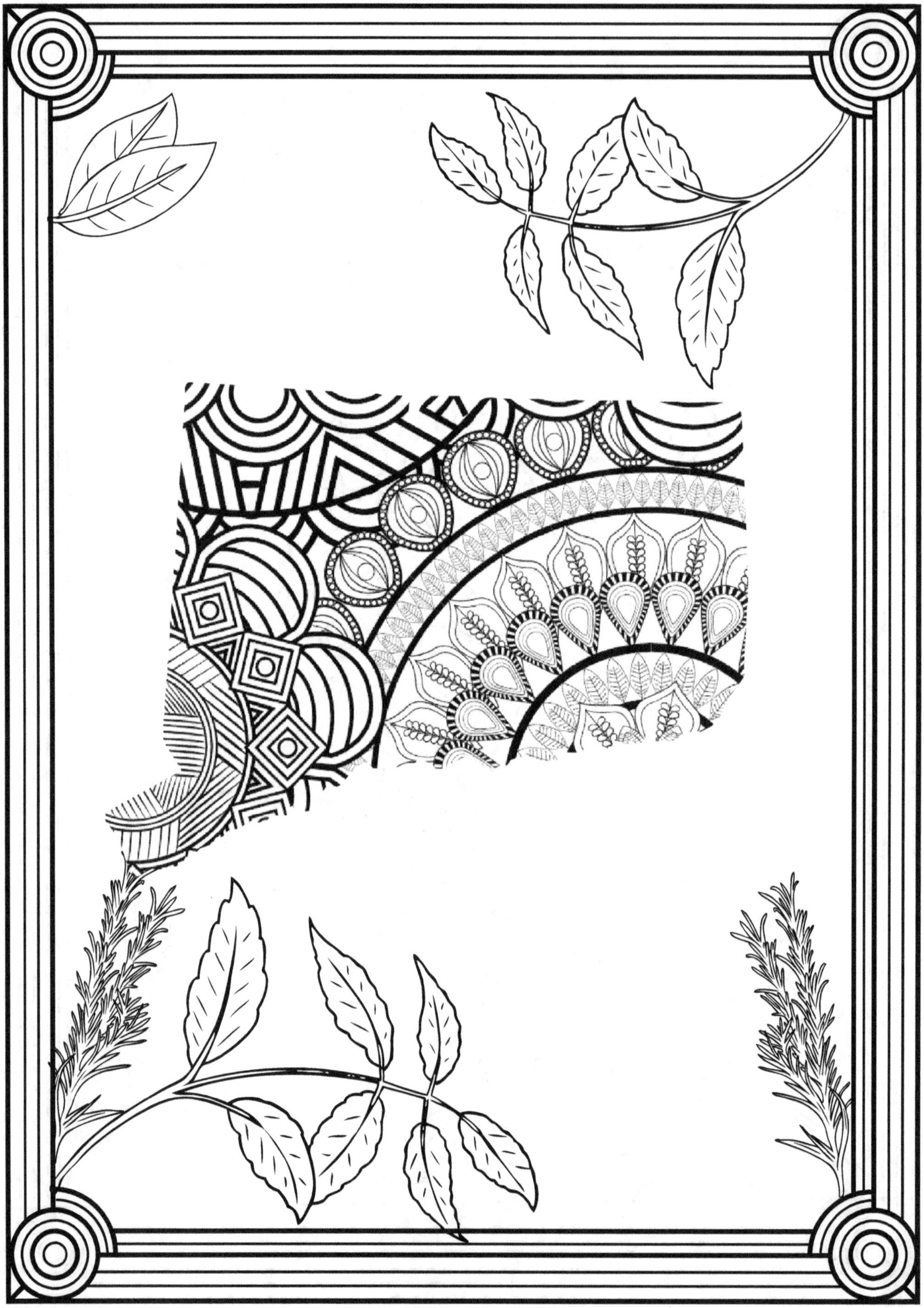

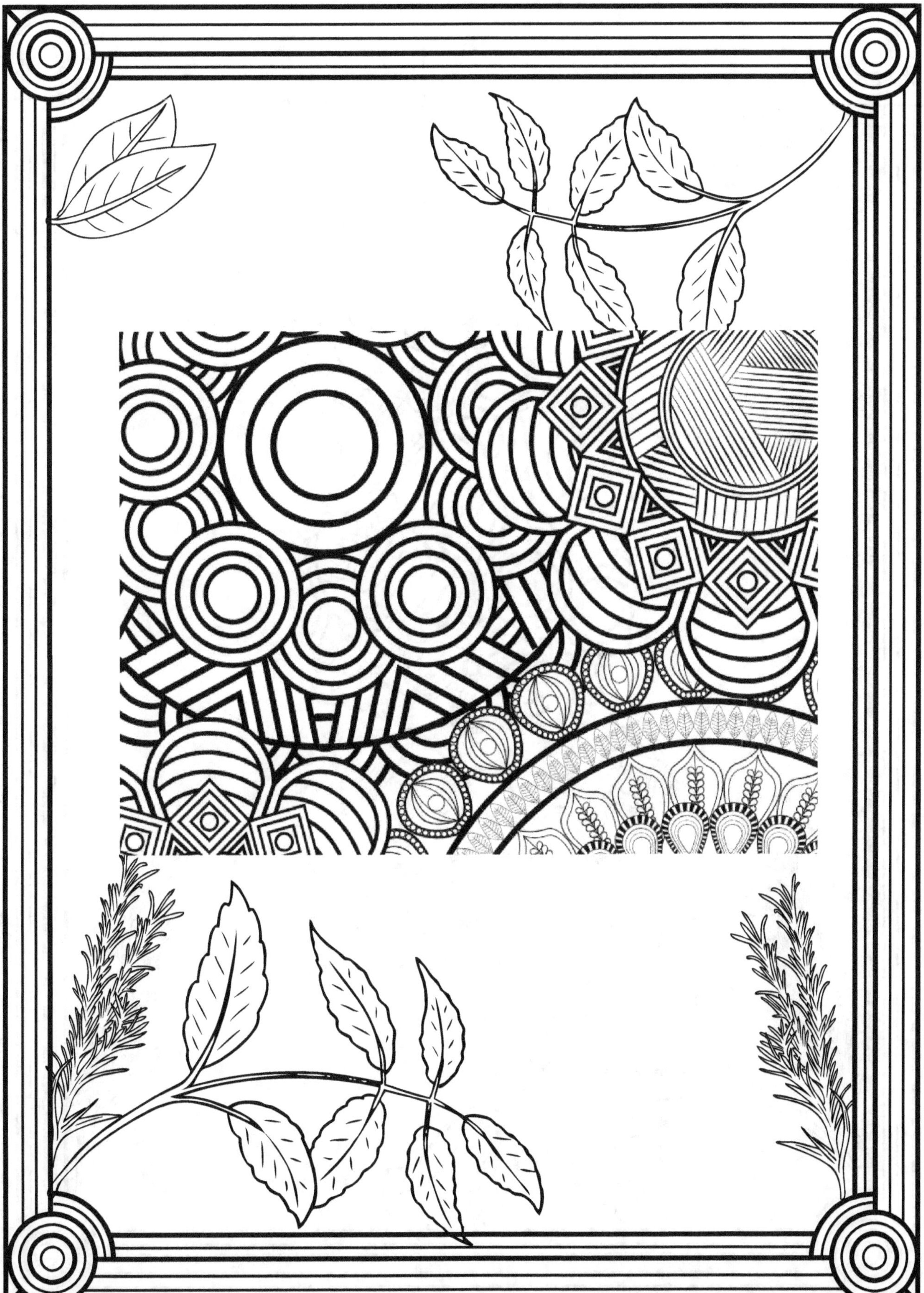

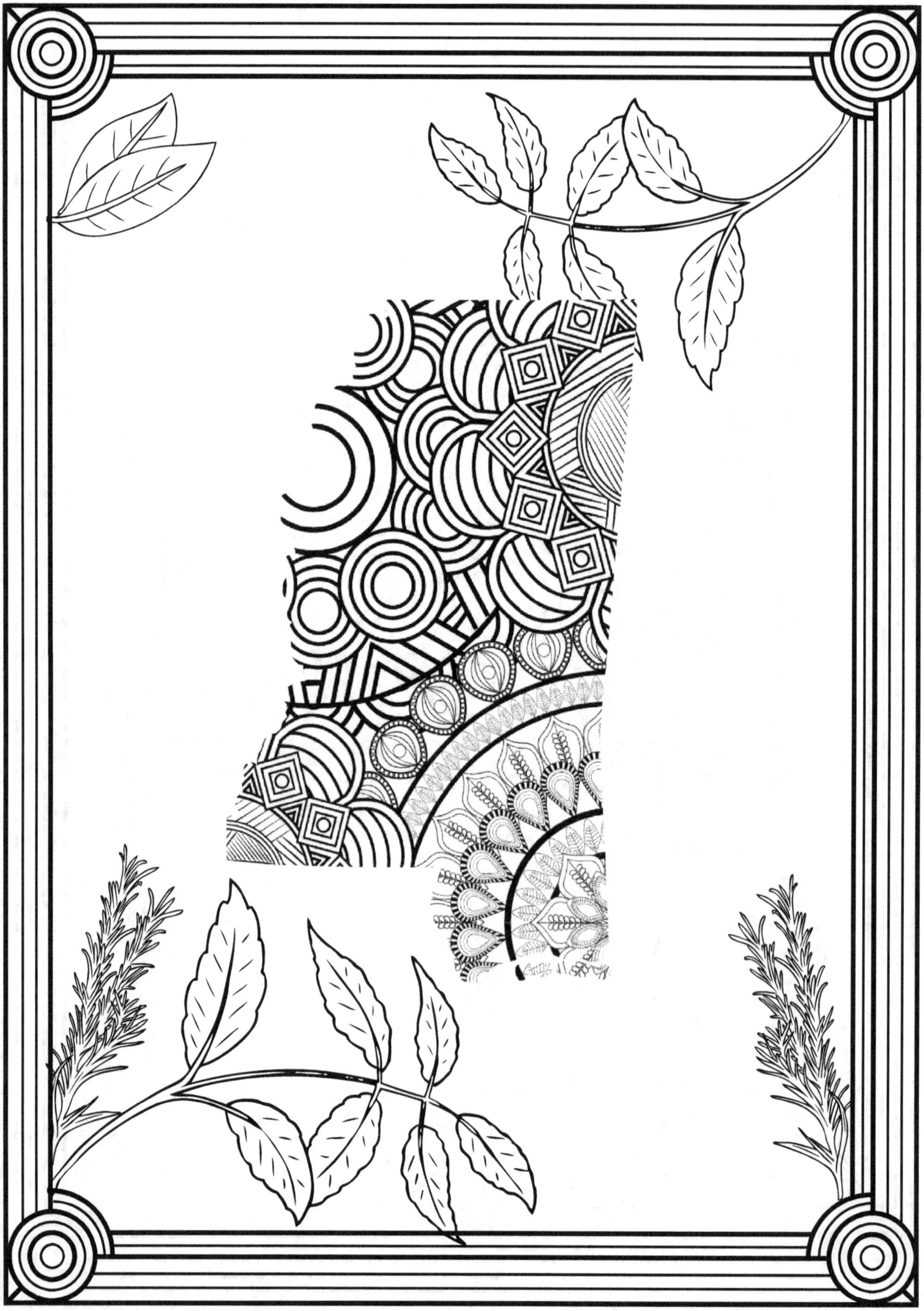

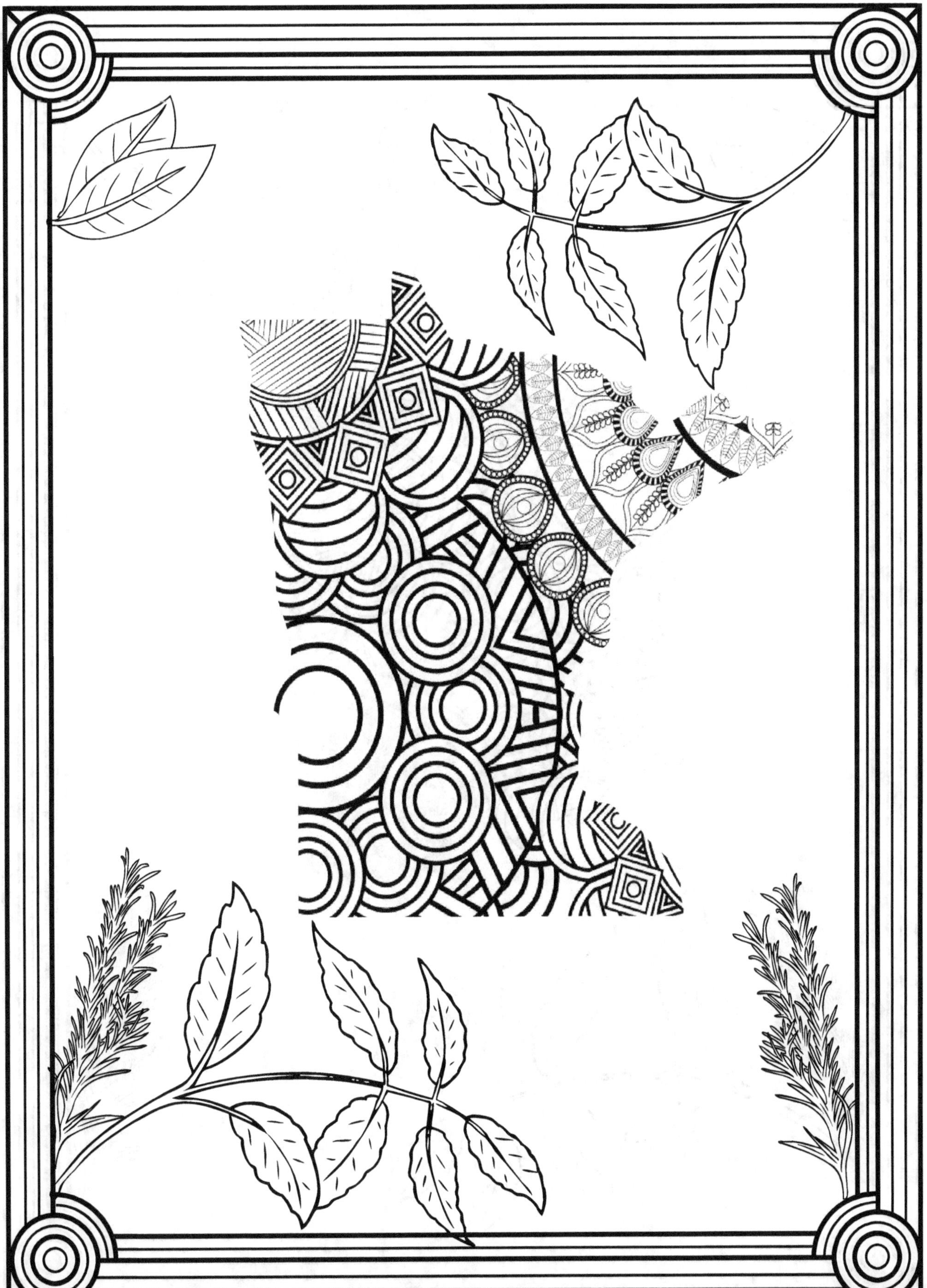

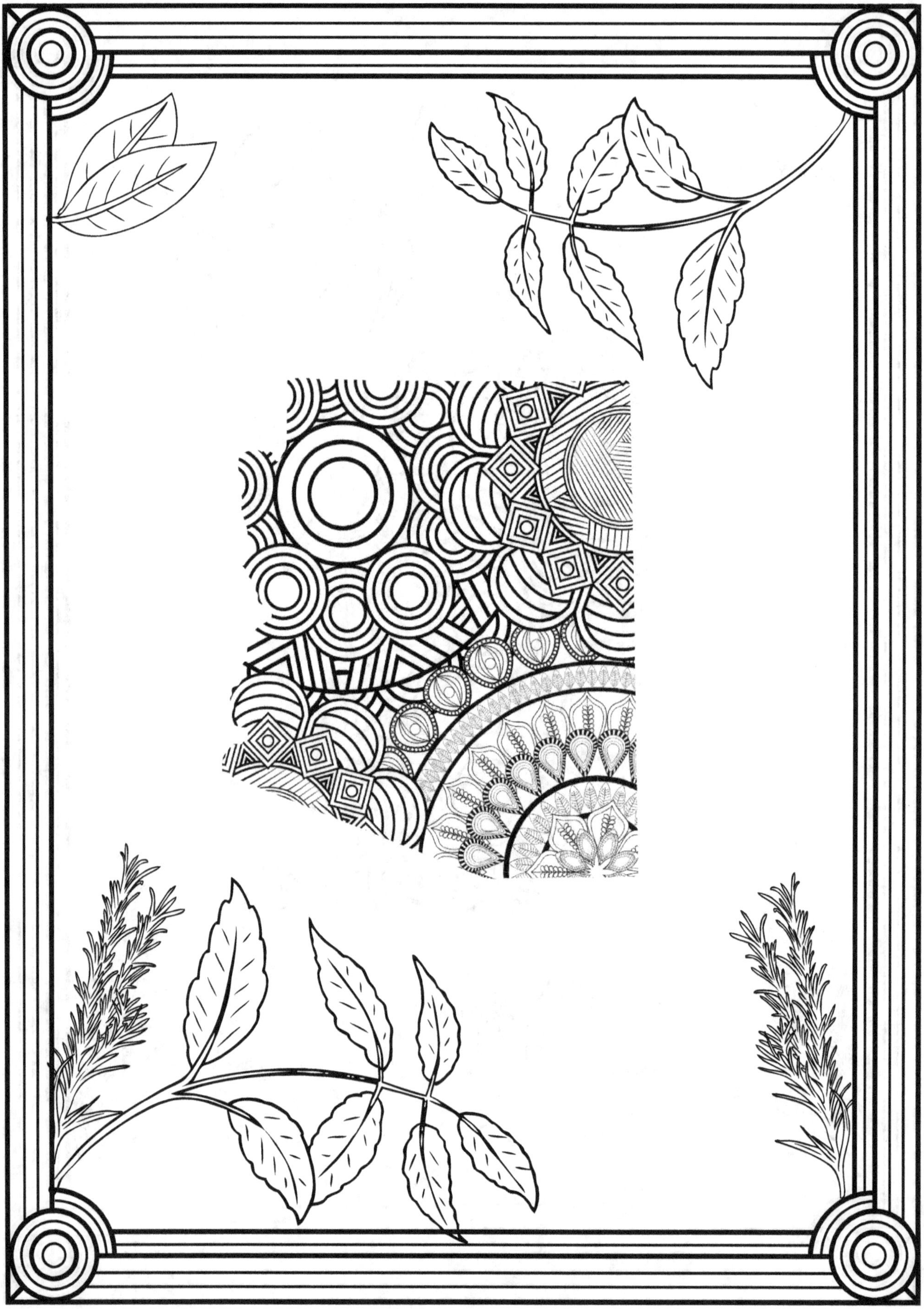

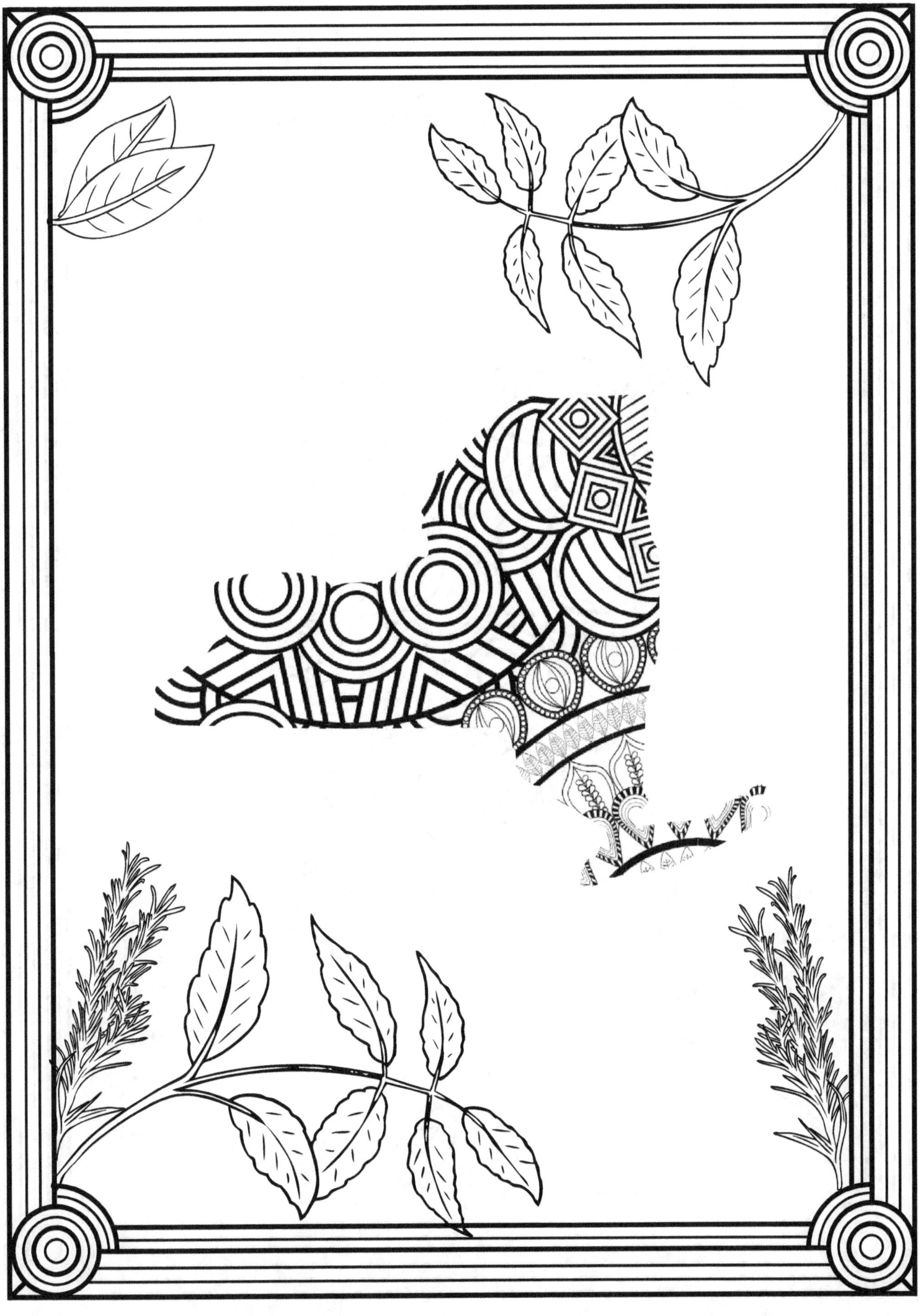

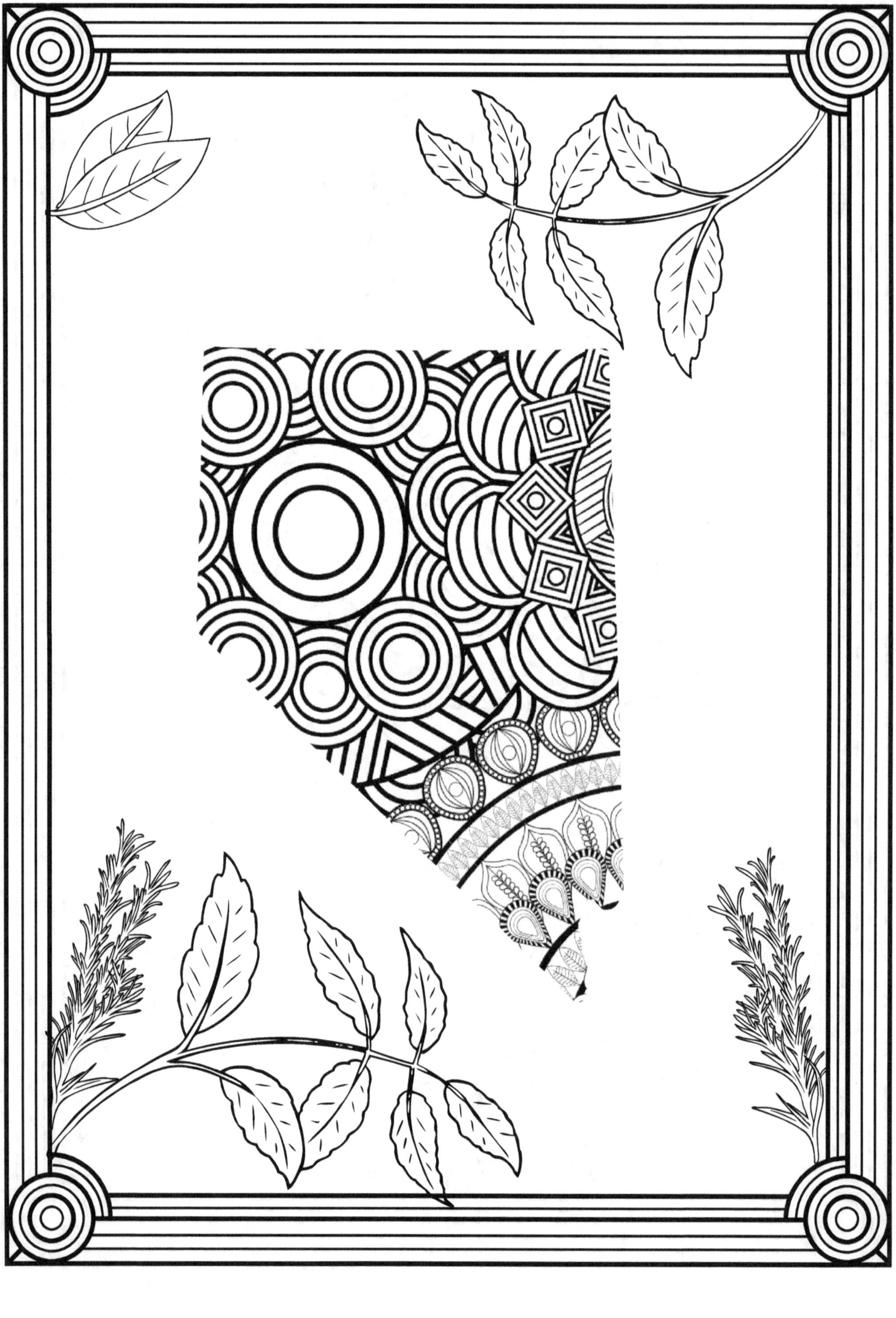

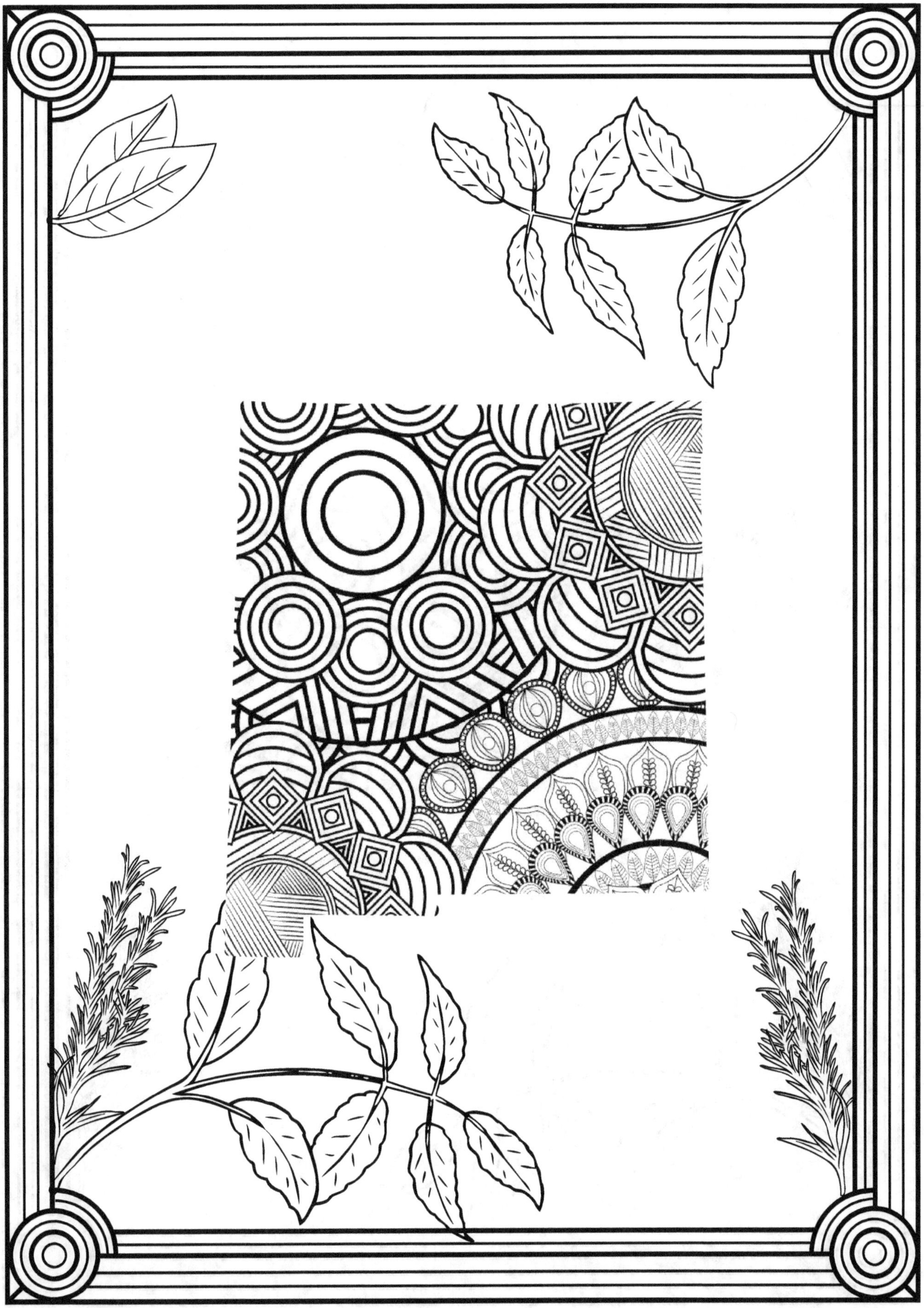

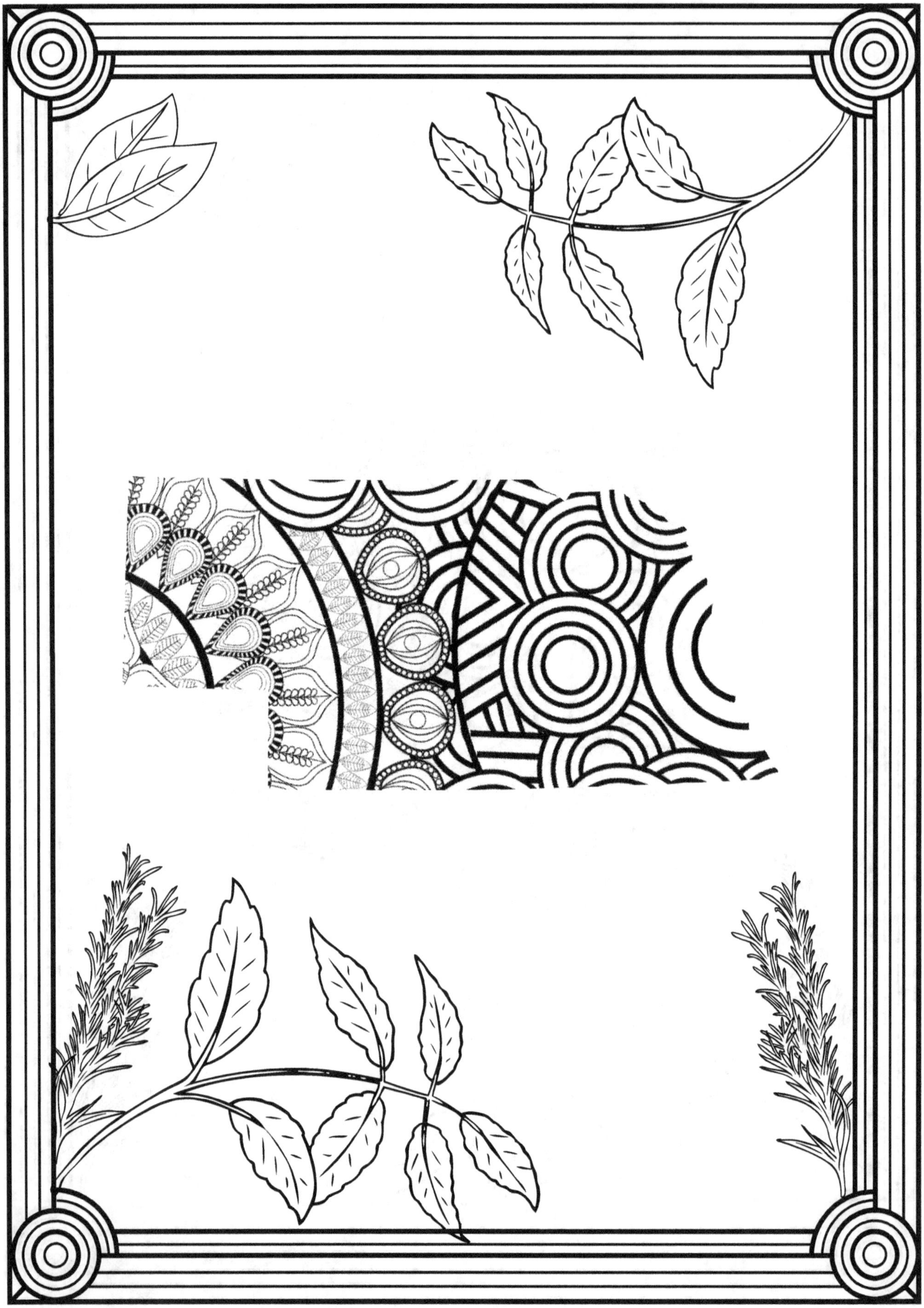

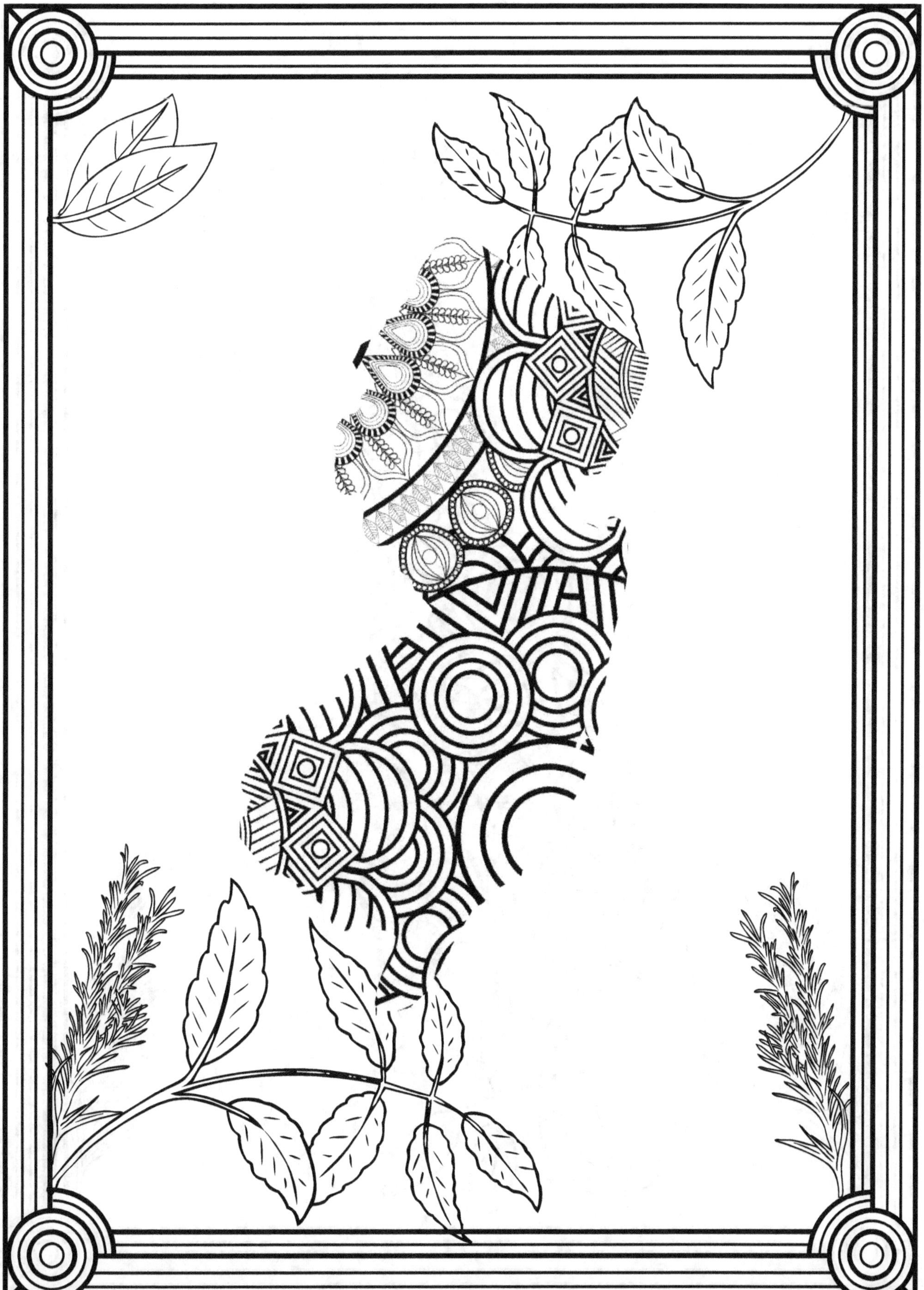

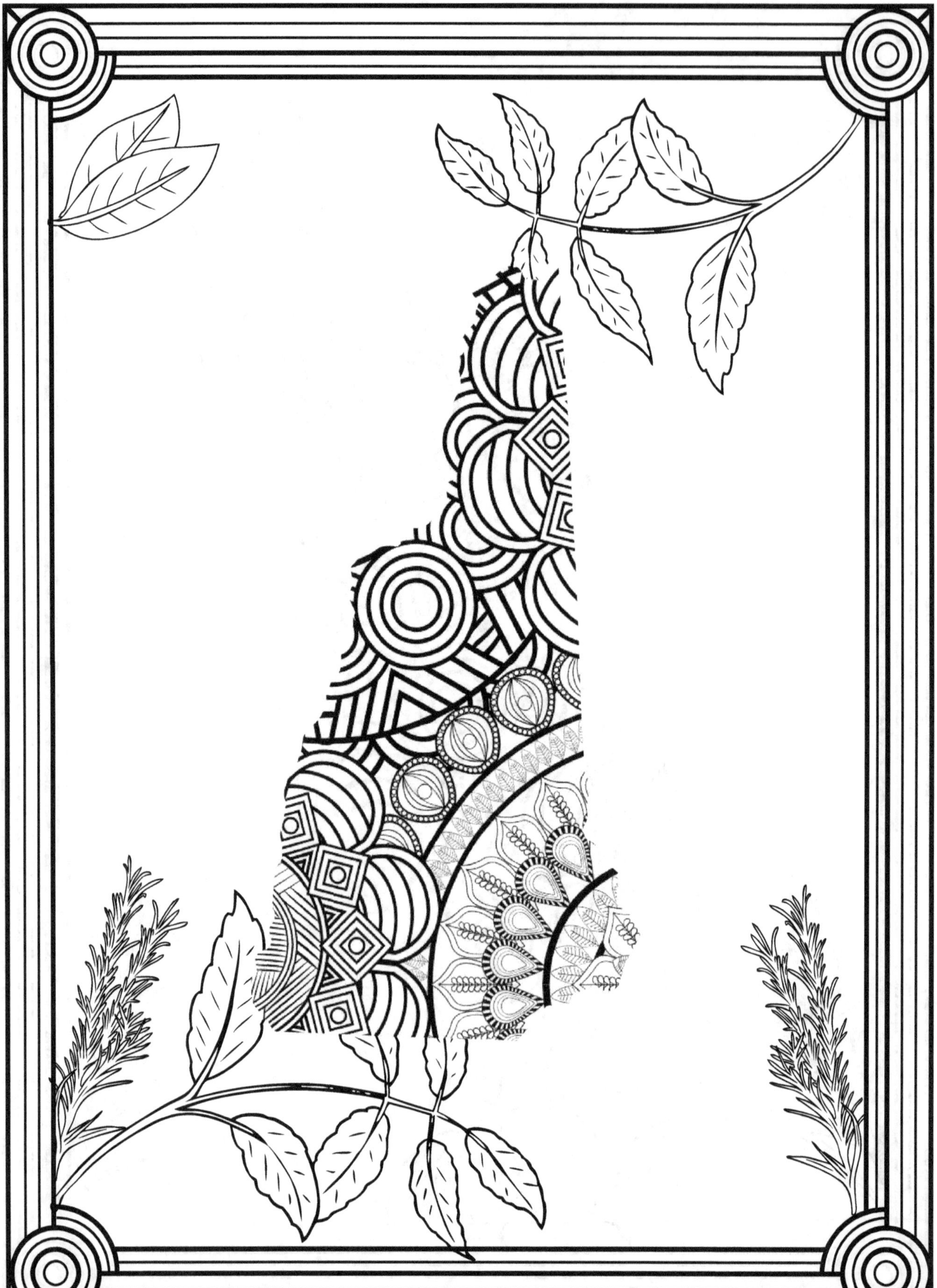

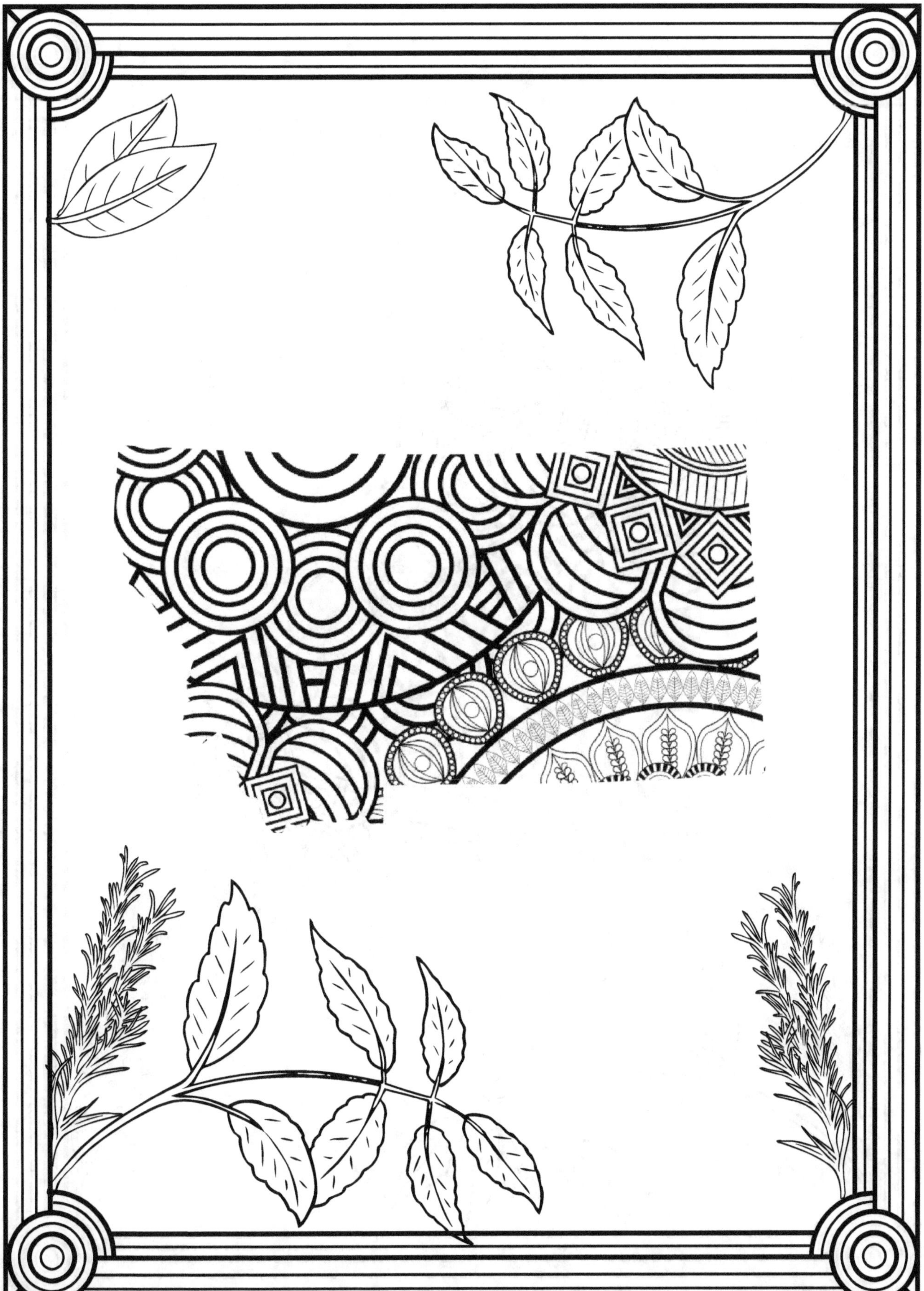

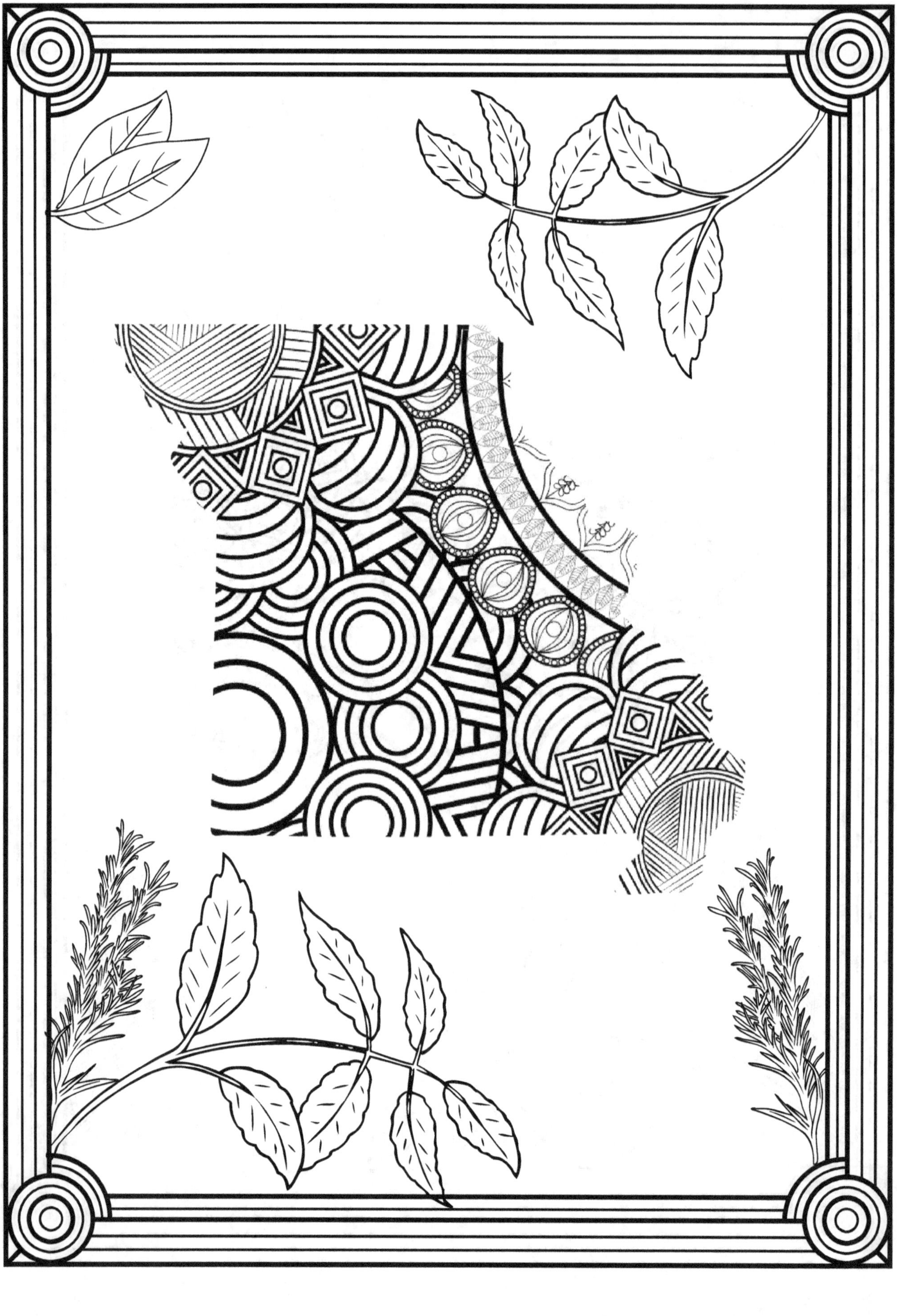

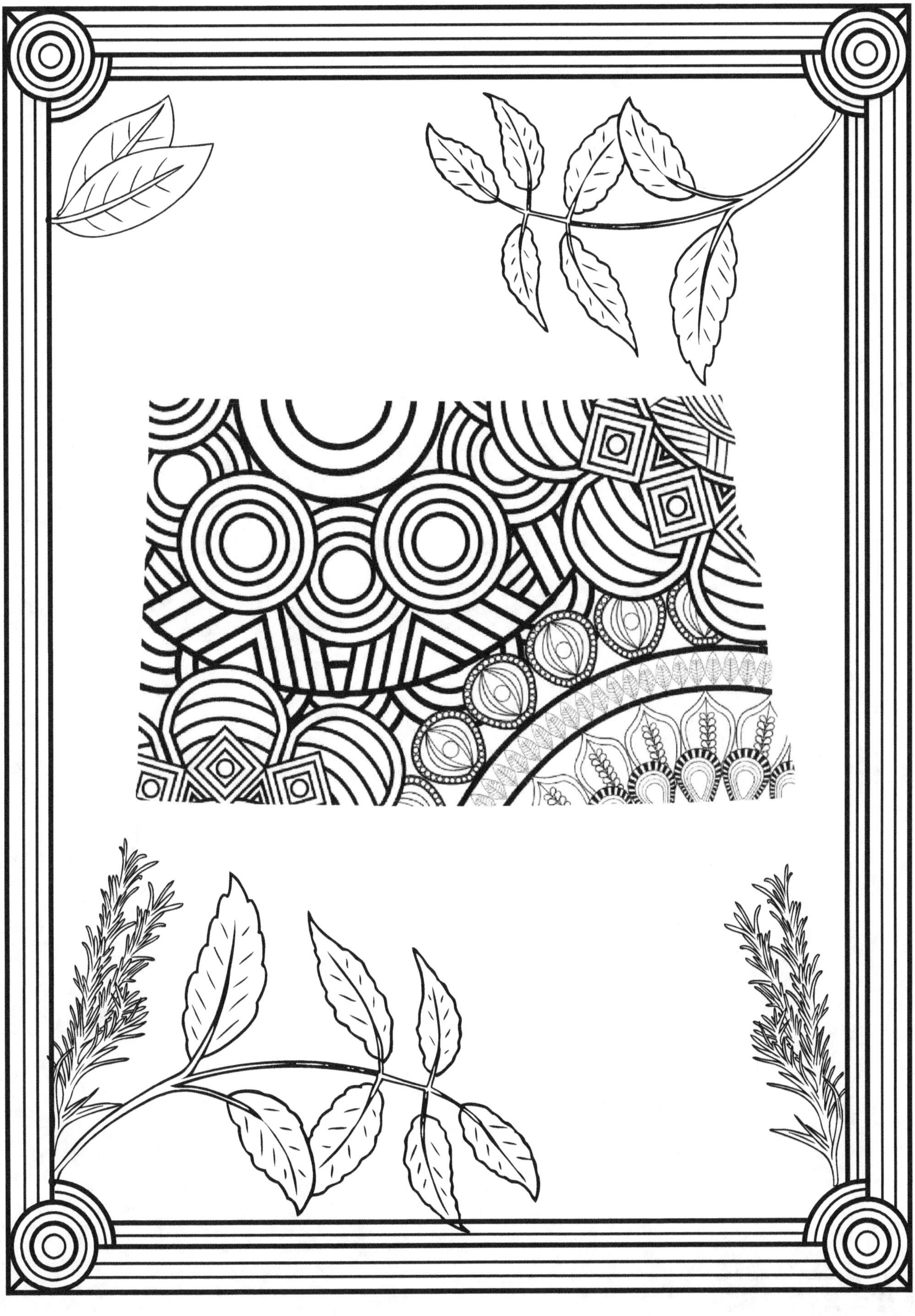

www.ingramcontent.com/pod-product-compliance
Lightning Source LLC
Chambersburg PA
CBHW080847170526
45158CB00009B/2663
* 9 7 8 1 0 7 1 1 0 3 1 7 3 *